Dedication

To all those who ever struggled with learning a foreign language and
to Wolfgang Karfunkel

Also by Yatir Nitzany

Conversational Spanish Quick and Easy

....

Conversational French Quick and Easy

....

Conversational Italian Quick and Easy

....

Conversational Portuguese Quick and Easy

....

Conversational German Quick and Easy

....

Conversational Dutch Quick and Easy

....

Conversational Norwegian Quick and Easy

....

Conversational Danish Quick and Easy

....

Conversational Russian Quick and Easy

....

Conversational Ukrainian Quick and Easy

....

Conversational Bulgarian Quick and Easy

....

Conversational Polish Quick and Easy

....

Conversational Heew Quick and Easy

....

Conversational Yiddish Quick and Easy

....

Conversational Armenian Quick and Easy

....

Conversational Romanian Quick and Easy

....

Conversational Arabic Quick and Easy

....

CONVERSATIONAL YIDDISH QUICK AND EASY SERIES

The Most Innovative Technique
To Learn the Yiddish Language

PART - 1, PART – 2, PART - 3

YATIR NITZANY

Translated by:
Pamela Russ

Foreword

About Myself

For many years I struggled to learn Spanish, and I still knew no more than about twenty words. Consequently, I was extremely frustrated. One day I stumbled upon this method as I was playing around with word combinations. Suddenly, I came to the realization that every language has a certain core group of words that are most commonly used and, simply by learning them, one could gain the ability to engage in quick and easy conversational Spanish.

I discovered which words those were, and I narrowed them down to three hundred and fifty that, once memorized, one could connect and create one's own sentences. The variations were and are *infinite*! By using this incredibly simple technique, I could converse at a proficient level and speak Spanish. Within a week, I astonished my Spanish-speaking friends with my newfound ability. The next semester I registered at my university for a Spanish language course, and I applied the same principles I had learned in that class (grammar, additional vocabulary, future and past tense, etc.) to those three hundred and fifty words I already had memorized, and immediately I felt as if I had grown wings and learned how to fly.

At the end of the semester, we took a class trip to San José, Costa Rica. I was like a fish in water, while the rest of my classmates were floundering and still struggling to converse. Throughout the following months, I again applied the same principle to other languages—French, Portuguese, Italian, and Arabic, all of which I now speak proficiently, thanks to this very simple technique.

This method is by far the fastest way to master quick and easy conversational language skills. There is no other technique that compares to my concept. It is effective, it worked for me, and it will work for you. Be consistent with my program, and you too will succeed the way I and many, many others have.

CONTENTS

The Yiddish Language

Written with Hebrew alphabet characters, Yiddish is a High German language that was used by Jews from central and Eastern Europe before the Holocaust. Most likely beginning around the ninth century CE, Yiddish was developed over the course of several centuries by Ashkenazi Jews in the Holy Roman Empire. Yiddish combined a Germanic language base with some Aramaic, Hebrew, Slavic, and even a smattering of Romance language words to create a distinct patois that served to unite diverse Jewish populations in Europe following the Diaspora. As Jewish communities grew in Europe, the Yiddish language grew with them, eventually including as many as ten to thirteen million speakers. However, the deaths of six million Jews in the Holocaust and the subsequent dispersal of Jewish communities following World War II decimated the ranks of Yiddish speakers in the twentieth century, and currently, it is estimated that as few as two million people worldwide still speak Yiddish. Nonetheless, some Yiddish words have been absorbed by many of the languages with which Yiddish cultures interacted following World War II (including chutzpah, glitch, kitsch, klutz, kosher, schtum, schmooze, and verklempt, among others, in English). Today, the language is enjoying a resurgence in Hasidic Jewish communities where it is the primary language spoken.

Memorization Made Easy

There is no doubt the three hundred and fifty words in my program are the required essentials in order to engage in quick and easy basic conversation in any foreign language. However, some people may experience difficulty in the memorization. For this reason, I created Memorization Made Easy. This memorization technique will make this program so simple and fun that it's unbelievable! I have spread the words over the following twenty pages. Each page contains a vocabulary table of ten to fifteen words. Below every vocabulary box, sentences are composed from the words on the page that you have just studied. This aids greatly in memorization. Once you succeed in memorizing the first page, then proceed to the second page. Upon completion of the second page, go back to the first and review. Then proceed to the third page. After memorizing the third, go back to the first and second and repeat. And so on. As you continue, begin to combine words and create your own sentences in your head. Every time you proceed to the following page, you will notice words from the previous pages will be present in those simple sentences as well, because repetition is one of the most crucial aspects in learning any foreign language. Upon completion of your twenty pages, *congratulations,* you have absorbed the required words and gained a basic, quick-and-easy proficiency and you should now be able to create your own sentences and say anything you wish in the Yiddish language. This is a crash course in conversational Yiddish, and it works!

Conversational Yiddish Quick and Easy

The Most Innovative Technique
to Learn the Yiddish Language

Part I

YATIR NITZANY

Introduction to the Program

People often dream about learning a foreign language, but usually they never do it. Some feel that they just won't be able to do it while others believe that they don't have the time. Whatever your reason is, it's time to set that aside. With my new method, you will have enough time, and you will not fail. You will actually learn how to speak the fundamentals of the language—fluently in as little as a few days. Of course, you won't speak perfect Yiddish at first, but you will certainly gain significant proficiency. For example, if you visit Brooklyn or Yiddish speaking areas of Israel, you will almost effortlessly be able engage in basic conversational communication with the locals in the present tense and you will no longer be intimidated by culture shock. It's time to relax. Learning a language is a valuable skill that connects people of multiple cultures around the world—and you now have the tools to join them.

How does my method work? I have taken twenty-seven of the most commonly used languages in the world and distilled from them the three hundred and fifty most frequently used words in any language. This process took three years of observation and research, and during that time, I determined which words I felt were most important for this method of basic conversational communication. In that time, I chose these words in such a way that they were structurally interrelated and that, when combined, form sentences. Thus, once you succeed in memorizing these words, you will be able to combine these words and form your own sentences. The words are spread over twenty pages. In fact, there are just nine basic words that will effectively build bridges, enabling you to speak in an understandable manner (please see Building

Bridges, page 49). The words will also combine easily in sentences, for example, enabling you to ask simple questions, make basic statements, and obtain a rudimentary understanding of others' communications. I have also created Memorization-Made-Easy Techniques (See page 9) for this program in order to help with the memorization of the vocabulary. My book is mainly intended for basic present tense vocal communication, meaning anyone can easily use it to "get by" linguistically while visiting a foreign country without learning the entire language. With practice, you will be 100 percent understandable to native speakers, which is your aim. One disclaimer: this is *not* a grammar book, though it does address minute and essential grammar rules. Therefore, understanding complex sentences with obscure words in Yiddish is beyond the scope of this book.

People who have tried this method have been successful, and by the time you finish this book, you will understand and be understood in basic conversational Yiddish. This is the best basis to learn not only the Yiddish language but any language. This is an entirely revolutionary, no-fail concept, and your ability to combine the pieces of the "language puzzle" together will come with *great* ease, especially if you use this program prior to beginning a Yiddish class.

This is the best program that was ever designed to teach the reader how to become conversational. Other conversational programs will only teach you phrases. But this is the *only* program that will teach you how to create your *own* sentences for the purpose of becoming conversational.

The Program

Memorize the vocabulary:

I - E'ech איך
I am - E'ech bin איך בין
With you - Mit deer מיט דיר
With us - Mit untz מיט אונז
For you - Far deir פאר דיר
For you - *(formal)* Far ir פאר איר
Are you? Du bist? ?דו ביסט
You are - Bistu ביסטו
You - Du, דו
You - Di די
You - *(formal)* Ir איר
You - *(plural)* Alle אלע
From - Fin (galitziana) פין
From - Foon (litvak) פון

Sentences composed from the vocabulary you just learned"

I am from Germany
E'ech bin fin Deuchland
איך בין פון דייטשלאנד

Are you from Israel?
Du bist fun Yisroel?
?דו ביסט פון ישראל

I am with you
E'ech bin mit dier
איך בין מיט דיר

This is for you.
Duce iz far dier
דאס איז פאר דיר

*This *isn't* a phrase book! The purpose of this book is *solely* to provide you with the tools to create *your own* sentences!

With him - Mit eim מיט אים
With her - Mit eer מיט איר
Without him - Oon aim אן אים
Without them - Nisht mit zai נישט מיט זיי
Always - Shten'dik שטענדיק
This - Duce דאס
This is - Dus iz דאס איז
Is - Iz איז
It's - Es iz עס איז
Is it? - Iz es?? איז עס??
Sometimes – Am'oole אמאל
You are - Bistu ביסטו
Are you? - Du bist?? דו ביסט??
He - Er ער
She - Zi זי
Today – Haynt היינט

Are you at the house?
Bistu in shtub?
?ביסטו אין שטוב

I am always with her.
E'ech bin shten'dik mit eer
איך בין שטענדיק מיט איר

Are you alone today?
bistu heynt aleyn?
?ביסטו היינט אליין

Sometimes I go without him.
A mol gey ikh on im.
א. מאל גיי איך אן אים

Nisht mit literally means "not with."

14

Was - Gev'ain געווען
Was - Iz gev'ain איז געווען
I was - E'ech bin gev'ain איך בין געווען
To be - Tsu zain צו זיין
Good – Goot גוט
Here – Do דא
Very – Zeyer זייער
And – Un און
Between – Tsvishn צווישן
If – Oi'bb אויב
Now – Yetst יעצט
Tomorrow – Morgen מארגן
Where are you from? - Fin vi bista? פון ווי ביסטו?
How old are you? - Vi alt bistu? ?ווי אלט ביסטו

I was here with them
E'ech bein gev'ain do mit zei
איך בין געווען דא מיט זיי

You and I
Di un e'ech
די און איך

I was home at 5pm
ikh bin geven in der heym 5:00
איך בין געווען אין דער היים 5:00

Between now and tomorrow.
Tsvishn itst aun morgn.
צווישן איצט און מארגן.

Where are you from?
Fuhn vanet bistu?
פון וואנעט ביסטו?

How old are you?
Vi alt bistu?
?ווי אלט ביסטו

The – Di די

A - Ein אן

A - A א

Later - Shpeter שפעטער

After - Noch נאך

Afterwards – Nochdem נאכדעם

Yes – Yo יא

To – Tsu צו

Person - Mentsh מענטש

Happy – Gliklech גליקלעך

Happy – Tsufridn צופרידן

Better – Besser בעסער

Day – Toog טאג

Tomorrow – Morgen מארגן

Then – Demolt דעמאלט

Good morning - Gutt Morgen גוט מארגן

How are you? - Vas machstu? וואס מאכסטו

Today – Haynt היינט

It's better to be home later.

Es iz beser tsu kumen aheym shpet.

עס איז בעסער צו קומען אהיים שפעטער.

If this is good, then I am happy.

oyb dos iz gut, bin ikh tsufridn.

אויב דאָס איז גוט, בין איך צופרידן.

Yes, you are very good

Yo, di bist zeyer git

יא, די ביסט זייער גיט

The same day

Di zelbe toog

די זעלבע טאג

Good morning, how are you today?

Gut morgn, vas machstu haynt?

גוט מארגן וואס מאכסטו היינט?

Where - Vu וואו
Where - Vi ווי
Ok – Okay אקאי
Everything - Alles אלעס
Everything - Alts אלץ
Somewhere – Ergets ערגעץ
Maybe - Efsher אפשר
What - Vus? וואס?
Almost – Shir nisht שיר נישט
There – Dort דארט
I go - E'ech gei איך גיי
Worse - Erger ערגער
Even if - Afil'e אפילו
No - Nein ניין

This is for us.
dos iz far undz.
דאָס איז פֿאַר אונדז.

Even if I go now
Afil'e oi'b e'ech gei yetst
אפילו אויב איך גיי יעצט

What? I am almost there
Vus? Eech bin bald dort
וואס? איך בין באלד דארט

Where are you?
Vu bist du?
ווי ביסטו?

Where is everything?
Vi iz alles?
ווי איז אלעס

Maybe somewhere
Efsher ergets
אפשר ערגעץ

Already – Shoin שוין
Son – Zun זון
Daughter – Tochter טאכטער
To have - Tsu hoben צו האבן
Doesn't - Nisht נישט
Hard - Shver שווער
Easy - Lae'echt לייכט
Still – Doch דאך
Impossible - Aummeglekh אוממעגלעך
House - Hoyz הויז
House - shteeb שטיב
Home - Haym היים
In, at, at the, in the - In אין
In, at, at the, in the - Bai ביי
Car - Vugen וואגן
Car - Auto אויטא
Car - Mashin מאשין
Book - Buch בוך
He is - Er iz ער איז
She is - Zi iz זי איז
Isn't – Iz nisht איז נישט

She is not in the car, so maybe she is still at the house?
zi iz nit in oyto, iz efsher iz zi nokh in hoyz
?זי איז ניט אין אויטא ,איז אפשר איז זי נאך אין הויז

I am already in the car with your son and your daughter
E'ech bein shoiin in auto mit deyn zun aun deyn tochter
איך בין שוין אין אויטא מיט דיין זין און דיין טאכטער

This is very hard, but it's not impossible
Dos iz zeyer shver, ober es iz nisht aummeglekh
דאָס איז זייער שווער ,אָבער עס איז נישט אוממעגלעך

Thank you – A sheinem dank אַ שיינעם דאַנק
Thanks – A dank אַ דאַנק
For – Far פֿאַר
Anything – Alles אַלעס
That - Duce דאָס
That is - Duce iz דאָס איז
But/however - Ober אָבער
No - Nein ניין
Not - Nisht נישט
I am not - E'ech bin nisht איך בין נישט
Away – Avek אַוועק
Same / like *(as in similar)* **–** Zelbe זעלבע
Like (preposition) **–** Vi ווי

Thank you, David.
A dank, Dovid.
אַ. דאַנק, דוד.

It's almost time
Ez iz shi'er der tsa'yt
עס איז שיער דער צייט

I am not here, I am far away
ikh bin nisht do, ikh bin vayt avek
איך בין נישט דאָ, איך בין ווייַט אַוועק

That house is similar to ours.
dos hoyz iz enlekh tsu unzers.
דאָס הויז איז ענלעך צו אונדזערס.

*In Yiddish there are 3 definitions for "time":
Time - Tsa'yt צייט (reference to; hour, "what time is it?")
Time - Tseyt צייט (era, moment period, duration of time)
Time – Mol מאָל (occasion or frequency)

*This *isn't* a phrase book! The purpose of this book is *solely* to provide you with the tools to create *your own* sentences!

I say / I am saying - E'ech zoog איך זאג

What time is it? - Vos iz der tsa'yt וואס איז דער צייט

I want - E'ech vil איך וויל

Without you - Oo'n dir אן דיר

Everywhere /wherever – Uberall איבעראל

I am going - E'ech gey איך גיי

With – Mit מיט

My – Mein מיין

Light - Le'echt לייכט

I need - E'ech darf איך דארף

I see / I am seeing - E'ech zei איך זע

Right now - Yetst יעצט

I am saying no / I say no
E'ech zoog az nisht
איך זאג אז נישט

You need to be at home.
Du darfst zayn in shtub.
דו דארפסט זיין אין שטוב

I see light outside
E'ech zei le'echt in draussen
איך זע ליכט אין דרויסן

What time is it right now?
Vos iz du tsa'yt yetst?
וואס איז די צייט יעצט?

I see this everywhere
E'ech zei duce uberall
איך זע דאס איבעראל

I want this car
E'ech vil duce mashin
איך וויל דאס מאשין

To see – Tzu zein צו זעהן
Outside - Droissen דרויסן
Outside - Aroys ארויס
Without - Oo'n אן
Cousin - Kuzin קוזין
Cousin - (P)Kusinkes קוזינקעס
Happy – Gliklech גליקלעך
Happy – Tsufridn צופרידן
Another/ other - Ander'e אנדערע
Side – Zayt זייט
Until – Biz ביז
Yesterday – Nachten נעכטן
Without us - Nisht mit untz נישט מיט אונז
Since - Vayl ווייל
Since - Zint זינט
Day – Toog טאג
Before – Frier פריער
Late - Shpate שפעט

But I was here until late yesterday
Ober eech bin gevain du biz shpate nachten
אבער איך בין געוװען דא ביז שפעט נעכטן

Since the other day
Zint di ander'e toog
זינט די אנדערע טאג

I want to see this in the daytime
E'ech vil zen duce bai toog
איך וויל דאס זען ביי טאג

I am happy without any of my cousins here
ikh bin tsufridn on keyn fun mayne shvesterkinder do
איך בין צופרידן אָן קיין פון מַײנע שוועסטערקינדער דאָ

21

Easy - Lae'echt לייכט
To find - Tsu gefinen צו געפינען
To look for/to search - Tsu ze'echen צו זיכן
To wait - Tsu varten צו ווארטן
To sell - Tsu farkoifen צו פארקויפן
To use - Tsu nitsen צו ניצן
To know - Tsu visn צו וויסן
To decide - Tsu bashlusn צו באשליסן
Both – Beyde ביידע
Night – Nacht נאכט

This place is easy to find
Duce platz iz lae'echt tsu gefinen
דאס פלאץ איז לייכט צו געפינען

I am saying to wait until tomorrow
E'ech zag tsu varten biz morgen
איך זאג צו ווארטן ביז מארגן

It's easy to sell this table
Es iz lae'echt tsu farkoyfn duce tish
עס איז לייכט צו פארקויפן דאס טיש

I want to use this
E'ech vil duce nitsen
איך וויל דאס ניצן

Where is the book?
vu iz der bukh?
וווּ איז דער בוך?

I need to look for you at the mall.
ikh darf dikh zukhn in mol.
איך דאַרף דיך זוכן אין מאָל.

I need to be there at night
E'ech darf zayn dort ba nacht
איך דארף זיין דארט ביי נאכט

Place – Platz פלאץ
Because – Vayl ווייל
Them, they - Zey זיי
Their - Zeyer זייער
Bottle – Flashe פלאש
Mine – Mayn מיין
Myself – Zich זיך
To understand – Tsu farshteyn צו פארשטיין
Problem - Problem פראבלעם
Problems – Problemen פראבלעמען
I do, I am doing - E'ech mach איך מאך
I do, I am doing - E'ech ti איך טי
Of – Foon פון
To look - Tsu kuken צו קוקן
To do - Tsu tin צו טין
To do - Tsu ton צו טאן
Near - Leiben לעבן
Close - Nuent נאנט

Is this place near?
iz dos ort noent?
?איז דאָס אָרט נאָענט

I do what I want.
ikh tu vos ikh vil.
.איך טו וואָס איך וויל

That book is mine.
Dos iz mayn bukh
דאָס איז מיַין בוך

I need to understand the problem
E'ech darf farshteyn der problem
איך דארף פארשטיין דער פראבלעם

Enough - Genug גענוג
To buy - Tsu koyfen צו קױפֿן
Food - Essen עסען
Water - Vasser װאסער
Each/ every - Yay'den יעדן
Each/ every - Yeder יעדער
Everything - Alles אלעס
Everything - Alts אלץ
Everybody / Everyone - Yederin יעדערן
Everybody / Everyone - Alemen אלעמען
Hotel – Hotel האָטעל

I like this hotel because it's near the beach
ikh hob lib dem hotel vayl es iz lebn dem breg
איך האָב ליב דעם האָטעל ווייַל עס איז לעבן דעם ברעג

I want to look at the view.
ikh vil kukn afn oysblik
איך וויל קוקן אויפֿן אויסבליק.

I want to buy a bottle of water
E'ech vil koyfen a flashe vaser
איך וויל קויפֿן א פֿלאש װאסער

Do it like this!
tu es azoy
טו עס אזוי

Both of them have enough food
Beyde foon zey hoben genug essen
ביידע פֿון זיי האבן געניג עסן

I have a view of the city from the hotel
Fin di hotel e'ech hob an oisblik foon di shtut
פֿון די האָטעל האָב איך אן אויסבליק פֿון די שטאט

There isn't enough time to go to Brooklyn today
Heynt iz nisht genug tseyt tsu geyn keyn bruklin
היינט איז נישט גענוג צייַט צו גיין קיין ברוקלין

I like – E'ech glach איך גלייך
Family – Mishpuch'e משפחה
Parents – Eltern עלטערן
Why - Vuss וואס
Why - Far vuss פאר וואס
To say - Tsu zogn צו זאגן
Something – Epes עפעס
To go - Tsu geyn צו גיין
To work - Zu arbeiten צו ארבייטן
Who – Ver ווער
Important - Ve'echtik וויכטיג
Hello – Hi היי
What is your name? - Vus iz deyn numen? ?וואס איז דיין נאמען
Your – Deyn דיין

Hello, what is your name?
Hi, vos iz deyn nomen?
?היי, וואס איז דיין נאמען

I like to be at home with my parents
E'ech glach tsu zeyn in shtyb mit meyne eltern
איך גלייך צו זיין אין שטיב מיט מיינע עלטערן

Why do I need to say something important?
farvos darf ikh zogn epes vikhtik?
?פֿארוואָס דֿארף איך זאָגן עפעס וויכטיק

I am there with him
E'ech bin dort mit aim
איך בין דארט מיט עם

I like to work
E'ech glach tsu arbeiten
איך גלייך צו ארבעטן

Who is there?
Ver iz dort?
ווער איז דארט

To know - Tsu visn צו וויסן

There is - Es iz עס איז

There are - Es zenen עס זענען

Ready – Greyt גרייט

Soon – Balt באלד

That *(conjunction)* – Az אז

Busy – Farnumen פארנומען

How much /How many- Vi fil ווי פיל

To bring - Tsu brengen צו ברענגען

With me - Mit mir מיט מיר

Cold – Kalt קאלט

Inside – In אין

It is very cold in the library
Si zeyer kalt in der biblyotek
עס איז זייער קאלט אין דער ביבליאטעק

I am busy, but I need to be ready soon
E'ech bin farnumen, ober e'ech darf tsu zeyn greyt balt
איך בין פארנומען אבער איך דארף זיין גרייט באלד

I want to know if they are here.
ikh vil visn tsi zey zenen da.
איך וויל וויסן צי זיי זענען דא.

I can go outside.
ikh ken aroys geyen.
איך קען ארויס גיין.

There are seven dolls
Es zenen do zibn lalkes.
עס זענען דא זיבן לאלקעס

I need to know that everything is okay
E'ech darf visn az alts iz g'it
איך דארף וויסן אז אלץ איז גיט

How much money do I need to bring with me?
vifil gelt darf ikh mitbrengen?
ווייפיל געלט דארף איך מיטברענגען?

Instead – Enshtot אנטשטאט
Only – Nor נאר
When – Ven ווען
I can - E'ech ken איך קען
Can I? - Ken e'ech? קען איך?
Or – Oder אדער
Were – Zenen זענען
Without me - Oo'n me'er אן מיר
To eat - Tsu essen צו עסן
To Drive - Tsu furen צו פארן
Fast – Shnel שנעל
Slow - Pamelach פּעמעלעך
Slow - Langsam לאנגזאם
Hot - Ha'ys הייס

I like bread instead of rice.
ikh hob lib broyt anshtot rayz.
איך האב ליב ברויט אנשטאט רייז

I can work today
E'ech ken arbeten haynt
איך קען ארבעטן היינט

Only when you can
Nor ven ir kent
נאר ווען איר קענט

Go there without me.
gey ahin on mir.
גיי אהין אן מיר.

I need to drive the car very fast or very slowly
E'ech darf firen di mashin zeyer shnel oder zeyer pamelach
איך דארף פירן די מאשין זייער שנעל אדער זייער פּאמעלעך

I like to eat a hot meal for my lunch.
ikh hob lib tsu esn a heyse moltsayt far meyn mitog.
איך האב ליב צו עסן א הייסע מאלצייט פאר מיין מיטאג

To answer - Tsu entfern צו ענטפערן
To fly - Tsu flee'en צו פליען
To travel - Arumtsuforn ארומצופארן
To learn - Tsu lernen צו לערנען
How – Vi ווי
To leave (something) - Tsu lozn צו לאזן
To leave (a place) - Geyen גייען
Many / much - Fil פיל
A lot - Asach אסאך
I go to - E'ech gey tsu איך גיי צו
First – Ershter ערשטער
World – Velt וועלט
Synagogue - Shul שול
Around – Arim ארום
To walk - Tsu ga'yn צו גיין
Yours - deyne דיינע

Since the first time
Zint di ershter mol
זינט די ערשטע מאל

The children are yours
Di kinder zenen deyne
די קינדער זענען דיינע

I need to answer many questions
E'ech darf entfern fil shailes
איך דארף ענטפערן פיל שאלות

I want to fly today
E'ech vil flee'en haynt
איך וויל פליען היינט

You need to walk around the house
Ir darft ga'yn arum dem shtyb
איר דארפט גיין ארום דעם שטוב

To swim - Tsu shvimen צו שווימען
To practice - Tsu praktiziren צו פראקטיצירן
To play - Tsu shpiln צו שפילן
Time - Tsa'yt צייט (reference to; hour, "what time is it?")
Time - Tseyt צייט (era, moment period, duration of time)
Time – Mol מאל (occasion or frequency)
How – Vi ווי
Better – Besser בעסער

Everything is about the money.
alts iz vegn gelt.
אַלץ איז וועגן געלט.

I want to leave my dog at home.
ikh vil lozn meyn hunt in shtub.
איך וויל לאָזן מיין הונט אין שטוב.

I want to travel the world.
ikh vil arumforn di velt.
איך וויל אַרומפאָרן די וועלט.

I need to learn to swim
E'ech darf lernen tsu shvimen
איך דארף לערנען צו שווימען

I want to learn how to play better tennis.
ikh vil lernen vi tsu shpiln beser tenis.
איך וויל לערנען ווי צו שפילן בעסער טעניס.

I am going to do my homework today
Ikh gey heynt makhn meyn heymarbet
איך גיי היינט מאכן מיין היימארבעט

*With the knowledge you've gained so far, now try to create your own sentences!

Nobody - Keinemen קיינעמן
Anyone - Keyner קיינער
Against – Kegen קעגן
Us – Untz אונז
To visit - Tsu furen צו פארן
Mom / Mother – Mame מאמע
To give - Tsu gebn צו געבן
Which – Vos וואס
Just – Nor נאר
Week – Voch וואך
Than – Vi ווי
Nothing – Gornisht גארנישט

Something is better than nothing
Epes iz beser vi gornisht
עפעס איז בעסער ווי גארנישט

I am against him
E'ech bin kegen ihm
איך בין קעגן אים

Do you do this every day?
Di machst duce yeden toog?
די מאכסט דאס יעדן טאג?

We go each week to visit my family
Mir geyn yeder voch tsu bezuchen meyn mishpuch'e
מיר גיין יעדער וואך צו באזוכן מיין משפחה

I need to give you something
E'ech darf gebn ir epes
איך דארף געבן איר עפעס

Ir is the formal "you." However, *ir* can also be used to demonstrate the indirect object pronoun of the pronoun "you," the person who is actually affected by the action that is being carried out. "I need to give you something" / *E'ech darf gebn ir epes* / איך דארף געבן איר עפעס

Towards – Tzu צו
Than – Vi ווי
To meet - Tsu trefn צו טרעפֿן
Someone – Emetser עמעצער
To walk - Tsu ga'yn צו גיין
Also / too / as well – Aoych אויך
Also / too / as well – Ochet אויכעט
Wednesday – Mitvoch מיטוואָך
Around – Arim ארום
To drink - Tsu trinken צו טרינקען
Woman – Froe פֿרוי
To begin / To start – On'tsuheiben אנצוהייבן
To finish - Tsu endikn צו ענדיקן

Do you want to meet someone?
Ir vilt trefn emetser?
איר ווילט טרעפֿן עמעצער?

I am here also on Wednesdays
Ee'ech bin do aioch yeden mitvoch.
איך בין דא אויך יעדן מיטוואך

You need to walk around the school.
ir darft geyn arum di shule.
איר דאַרפֿט גיין אַרום די שולע.

We want to start the class soon.
mir viln bald onheybn dem klas.
מיר ווילן באַלד אָנהייבן דעם קלאַס.

In order to finish at three o'clock this afternoon, I need to finish soon
kdi tsu endikn dray azeyger nokh mitog, darft ikh bald endikn
כדי צו ענדיקן דרײַ אַזייגער נאָך מיטאָג, דאַרפֿט איך באַלד ענדיקן

I have - E'ech hab איך האב
Don't – Nisht נישט
Friend – Fraynd פריינד
To borrow - Tsu borgn צו בארגן
To look like / resemble - Tsu kuken di zelba צו קוקן די זעלבע
Grandfather – Zeyde זיידע
To want - Tsu villn צו ווילן
To know - Tsu visn צו וויסן
To stay - Tsu blaybn צו בלייבן
To continue - Tsu forzetsn צו פארזעצן
Way (road, path) **-** Veig וועג
Way (road, path) **-** Strasse שטראסע
Way (road, path) **-** Avek אוועק
To do - Tsu tin צו טין
To do - Tsu ton צו טאן
School – shule שולע
On – Aoyf אויף

Why don't you have this book?
Farvuss hostanish duce be'yech?
פארוואס האסטו נישט דאס בוך

I want to borrow this book for my grandfather
E'ech vil borgn duce buch far meyn zeyde
איך וויל בארגן דאס בוך פאר מיין זיידע

This isn't the way to do this
Dos iz nisht der veg tsu ton dos
דאָס איז נישט דער וועג צו טאָן דאָס

I want to stay in New York because I have a friend there.
ikh vil bleybn in niu yark veyl ikh hob dort a khvr.
איך וויל בלייבן אין נעוו יארק ווייל איך האב דארט א חבר.

Our house is on the mountain.
undzer hoyz iz aoyf dem barg.
אונדזער הויז איז אויף דעם באַרג.

Anyone - Keyner קיינער

To look like / resemble - Tsu kuken di zelba צו קוקן די זעלבע

I don't - E'ech (verb) nisht איך (...)נישט

To show - Tsu vayzn צו ווייזן

To prepare - Tsugreytn צוגרייטן

To come - Tsu kumen צו קומען

About - Vegn וועגן

On the - Aoyf אויף

I did not go - E'ech bin nisht gegangen איך בין נישט געגאנגען

Do you want? - Di vilst? ?די ווילסט

Correct – Re'echtik ריכטיג

Do you want to look like Arnold
Di vilst oiszehn dezelba vi Arnold?
די ווילסט אויסזען די זעלבע ווי ארנאלד

I don't want to see anyone here
E'ech vil nisht zen keinamen do
איך וויל נישט זען קיינעמען דא

I need to show you how to prepare breakfast
E'ech darf vayzn auch vi tsu greytn frishtik
איך דארף ווייזן אייך ווי צו גרייטן פרישטיג

That is incorrect, I don't need the car today
Duce es nisht richdik, e'ech darf nisht di mashin haynt
דאס איז נישט ריכטיג, איך דארף נישט די מאשין היינט

I want to come with you.
Ikh vil kumen mit dir.
איך וויל קומען מיט דיר.

To remember - Tsu gedenken צו געדענקען
Your - Deyn דיין
Number – Numer נומער
Hour – Shuh שעה
Dark / darkness – Finster פינסטער
Grandmother – Bubbe באבע
Five - Fin'if פינף
Minute - Minet מיניט
More – Mehr מער
To think - Tsu trachtn צו טראכטן
To think - tracht טראכט
To hear - Tsu her'n צו הערן
Last - Let'ste לעצטע

I need to remember your number
E'ech darf gedenken deyn numer
איך דארף געדענקען דיין נומער

This is the last hour of darkness
Das iz di let'ste shoh foon fintsternish
דאס איז די לעצטע שעה פון פינצטערניש

I can hear my grandmother speaking Hebrew.
ikh ken hern mayn bobe redn hebreish.
איך קען הערן מײַן באבע רעדן העברעיִש.

I need to think about this more.
ikh darf nokh trakhtn vegn dem.
איך דארף נאָך טראַכטן וועגן דעם.

From here to there, it's only five minutes
Fin do tsu dorten, es iz nor fin'if minut
פון דא צו דארטן איז נאר פינף מינוט

Again - Nochamul נאכאמאל
Again - Vider ווידער
To take - Tsu nemen צו נעמען
To try - Tsu prubirn צו פראבירן
To rent - Tsu dingen צו דינגען
Without her - Oo'n eer אן איר
To turn off – Farleshen פארלעשן
To ask - Tsu fregn צו פרעגן
To stop - Tsu oifhalten צו האלטן
Early - Frie פרי
Beach – Yam ים
Tonight - Haynt ba nacht היינט ביי נאכט

I need to try this again
E'ech darf prubirn duce nochamul
איך דארף פראבירן דאס נאכאמאל

He must go and rent a house at the beach.
er muz geyn dingen a hoyz beym breg.
ער מוז גיין דינגען א הויז ביים ברעג.

We are here for a long time
Mir zenen do far a lange tseyt
מיר זענען דא פאר א לאנגע צייט

I need to turn off the lights early tonight
E'ech darf farleshen di le'echt frie haynt ba nacht
איך דארף פארלעשן די ליכט פרי היינט ביי נאכט

We want to stop here
Mir viln oifhaltn do
מיר ווילן אויפהאלטן דא

Permission – Derloybenish דערלויבעניש
Building - Bnin בנין
Doctor - Dokter דאָקטער
Exact – Pinktlech פינקטלעך
In order to - Veigen tsu וועגן צו
Airport - Flifeld פֿליפֿעלד
Sleep - Shlofn שלאָפֿן
Jerusalem - Yerushalayim ירושלים
We are - Mir zenen מיר זיינען

We are from Jerusalem.
Mir zenen fun Yerushalayim.
.מיר זענען פֿון ירושלים

Your doctor is in the same building.
deyn dokter iz in der zelbiker bnin.
.דיין דאָקטער איז אין דער זעלביקער בנין

In order to leave you have to ask permission.
tsu megn geyen darft ir betn derloybenish
צו מעגן גייען דאַרפֿט איר בעטן דערלויבעניש

Is it possible to know the exact date?
Iz es meglech tsu visn di pinktleche dateh?
?איז עס מעגלעך צו וויסן די פינקטלעכע דאטע

I want to go to sleep
Ikh vil geyn shlofn
איך וויל גיין שלאָפֿן

Where is the airport?
Vu iz der flifeld
?ווו איז דער פֿליפֿעלד

To open - Tsu efenen צו עפענען
A bit, a little, a little bit - A'bisel א ביסל
To pay - Tsu batsulen צו באצאלן
Sister – Shvester שוועסטער
To hope - Tsu hofen צו האפן
Name – Numen נאמען
Last name - Letste numen לעצטע נאמען
Door - Ti'er טיר
To get to know - Tsu bakenin צו באקענען
Future – Tsukunft צוקונפט
To buy - Tsu koyfen צו קויפן
Nice to meet you Es iz zeir sheiine tzi trefen deir
עס איז זייער שיין צו טרעפן דיר

I need to open the door for my sister
E'ech darf tsu efenen di tiyer far meyn shvester
איך דארף עפענען די טיר פאר מיין שוועסטער

I need to buy something
E'ech darf tsu koyfn epes
איך דארף קויפן עפעס

I want to meet your brothers.
ikh vil zikh trefn mit eyere brider.
איך וויל זיך טרעפן מיט אייערע ברידער.

We can hope for a better future.
mir kenen hofn aoyf a beseren tsukunft.
מיר קענען האפן אויף אַ בעסערען צוקונפֿט.

Nice to meet you, what is your name and your last name?
Es iz sheine tzi trefen deir, vos iz dein numen un deiner letste numen?
עס איז שיין צו טרעפן דיר, וואס איז דיין נאמען ,און וואס איז דיין לעצטע נאמען?

To happen - Tsu gesheyen צו געשען
To live - Tsu leiben צו לעבן
To return - Tsu gayn tzurik צו גיין צוריק
There isn't – Es iz nisht עס איז נישט
There aren't – Es zenen nisht עס זענען נישט
Why - Vuss וואס
Why - Far vuss פאר וואס
Sad – Troirig טרוריריק
Happy – Gliklech גליקלעך
Excuse me - Antshuldikn mir ענטשולדיקן מיר
Children – Kinder קינדער
To order - Tsu beshtelen צו בעשטעלן

It is impossible to live without problems.
es iz aummeglekh tsu lebn on problemen.
עס איז אוממעגלעך צו לעבן אָן פראבלעמען.

I want to return to the United States.
ikh vil tsurik geyenkeyn amerike.
איך וויל צוריק גייען קיין אמעריקע.

Why are you happy right now?
Farvuss bistu tzi'friden yetst?
פארוואס ביסטו צופרידן יעצט

This needs to happen today
Duce mizz gishayen haynt
דאס מיז געשעהן היינט

Excuse me, my child is here as well
Antshuldikt mir, meyn kind iz do ochet
ענטשולדיקט מיר, מיין קינד איז דא אויכעד

I want to order a soup.
ikh vil bashteln a zup.
איך וויל באַשטעלן אַ זופ.

To talk - Tsu reden צו רעדן

To speak - Shprechen צו שפרעכן

To help - Tsu helfn צו העלפֿן

To smoke - Tsu reychern צו רויכערן

To love - Tsu liben צו ליבן

Again - Nochamul נאכאמאל

Again - Vider ווידער

Yiddish – Yiddish יידיש

German – Deutsch דײַטש

How – Vi ווי

I want to learn how to speak perfect Yiddish and German.
ikh vil lernen vi azoy tsu redn perfekte yidish aun deutsh
איך וויל לערנען ווי אזוי צו רעדן פערפֿעקטע יידיש און דײַטש

I don't want to smoke again
E'ech vil'nisht reychern nochamul
איך וויל נישט רויכערן נאכאמאל

I want to help
E'ech vil helfen
איך וויל העלפֿן

I love you
E'ech hob dich lib
איך האב דיך ליב

I see you
E'ech zei dir
איך זע דיר

I need you
E'ech darf dir
איך דארף דיר

*"I love you" can also be *e'ech hob dir lib.*

39

To read - Tsu leynen צו לייַנען

To write - Tsu shrayben צו שרייַבן

To teach - Tsu lernen צו לערנען

To close – Tsu far'machen צו פֿאַרמאַכן

To choose - Tsu klayben צו קלייַבן

To prefer - Tsu vellen beser צו וועלן בעסער

To put - Tsu ley'gn צו לייגן

To put - Tsu shteln צו שטעלן

Less – Veyniker ווייניקער

Month – Choidesh חודש

I talk - E'ech red איך רעד

I need this book to learn how to read and write in Hebrew
ikh darf dos bukh tsu lernen vi azoy tsu leyenen aun shreybn aoyf hebreish
איך דאַרף דאָס בוך צו לערנען ווי אַזוי צו לייענען און שרייַבן אויף העברעאיש

I want to teach Yiddish in Israel.
ikh vil lernen yidish in Yisroel.
איך וויל לערנען ייִדיש אין ישראל.

I want to turn on the lights and close the door.
ikh vil ontsindn di likht un farmakhn di tir.
איך וויל אָנצינדן די ליכט און פֿאַרמאַכן די טיר.

I want to pay less than you.
ikh vil batsoln veyniker vi dir.
איך וויל באַצאָלן ווייניקער ווי דיר.

I prefer to put this here.
ikh vil es shteln do
איך וויל עס שטעלן דאָ

I speak with the boy and the girl in Yiddish
E'ech red mit dem yingel un di meydel oyf Yiddish
איך רעד מיט דעם ייִנגל און די מיידעל אויף ייִדיש

To exchange (*money***)** - Tsu vekslen צו וועקסלען

Money – Gelt געלט

To call - Tsu rufen צו ריפן

Brother – Brider ברודער

Dad – Tate טאטע

To sit - Tsu zitsen צו זיצן

Together – Tsuzamen צוזאמען

To change - Tsu toyshen צו טוישן

During – Be'eis בעת

Years - Yu'eren יארן

Sky – Himmel הימל

Sorry – Antshuldigt ענטשולדיקט

To the – Tsu di צו די

Big – Groys גרויס

Never / ever - Keynmol קיינמאל

I am never able to exchange this money at the bank.
ikh ken keynmol nish baytn dos gelt in der bank.
איך קען קיינמאָל נישט בײַטן דאָס געלט אין דער באַנק.

I want to call my brother and my dad today
E'ech vil rufen meyn bruder aun meyn tate haynt
איך וויל רופן מיין ברידער און מיין טאטע היינט

I am sorry.
Zay mir moykhl.
זײַ מיר מוחל

I need to put your cat on another chair
E'ech darf shteln deyn kats aoyf an andern shtul/benkel
איך דארף שטעלן דיין קאץ אויף אן אנדערן שטול /בענקל

*This *isn't* a phrase book! The purpose of this book is *solely* to provide you with the tools to create *your own* sentences!

Up – Aroyf אַרויף
Down – Aroop אַראָפ
Of course/certainly – Avadeh אוודאי
To follow - Tsu nochgeyn צו נאכגיין
New - Na'ye נייע
Dog - Hunt הונט
Welcome - Bruchim habaim ברוכים הבאים
Sun – Zin זין

Of course I can come to the theater, and I want to sit together with you and with your sister
Avadeh e'ech ken kimen tsum teater, aun e'ech vil zitzen tsuzamen mit deer un mit dein shvester
אוודאי קען איך קומען צו דעם טעאַטער, און איך וויל זיצן צוזאַמען מיט דיר און מיט דיין שוועסטער

If you look under the table, you can see the new rug.
aoyb ir kukt aunter dem tish, kent ir zen dem naye tepekh.
אויב איר קוקט אונטער דעם טיש, קענט איר זען דעם נײַען טעפּעך

I can see the sky from the window
E'ech ken zen der himmel foon di fentster
איך קען זען דער הימל פון די פענסטער

The dog wants to follow me to the store.
der hunt vil mir nochgeyen in kram.
דער הונט וויל מיר נאכגיין אין קראָם

There is sun outside today.
in droysn es iz zunik haynt
אין דרויסן עס איז זוניק הײַנט.

*With the knowledge you've gained so far, now try to create your own sentences!

To allow - Tsu lozn צו לאָזן
To believe - Tsu gloyben צו גלויבן
Morning - Frii פרי
Morning - Morgen מאָרגן
Except – Chuts חוץ
To promise – Tsu'tsuzugen צוצוזאָגן
Good night - Gutte nacht גוטע נאכט
To recognize - Tsu derkenen צו דערקענעןå
People – Mentshn מענטשן
Far – Vaytt ווייט
Him - Aim עם
His - Zeyn זיין
Her – Eer איר

I need to allow him to go with us.
ikh darf im lozn geyn mit aundz.
איך דאַרף אים לאָזן גיין מיט אונדז.

Come here quickly.
kum gikh aher.
קום גיך אַהער.

I can't recognize him.
ikh ken im nisht derkenen.
איך קען אים נישט דערקענען.

I believe everything except for this
Ikh gloyb alts akhuts dem
איך גלויב אַלץ אַחוץ דעם

I promise to say good night to my parents each night
Ikh zog tsu, tsu zogn a gute nakht tsu meyn eltern yeder nakht
איך זאָג צו צו זאָגן אַ גוטע נאַכט צו מיינע עלטערן יעדער נאַכט

Man – Mentsh אנדערש
To enter - Tsu arayngein צו אריינגיין
To receive - Tsu bakumen צו באקומען
Each, every – Yeder יעדער
Good day / afternoon - Gutten tog גוטן טאג
Afternoon – Nochmitoog נאכמיטאג
Left - Links לינקס
Right - Rechts רעכטס
To move (an object) - Tsu riren צו רירן
To move (to a place) – Tsu ibergein צו איבערגיין
Different – Andersh אנדערש
I Must - E'ech mizz איך מיז

He is a different man now.
er iz itst an ander mentsh.
.ער איז איצט אן אנדער מענטש

I must move my car to the right side of the street, because my sister needs to return home this afternoon
E'ech mizz mufen meyn mashin tsu di rechte zayt foon der gass, vayl meyn shvester darf kummen tzurik aheiym haynt nachmitoog.
איך מיז מופן מיין מאשין צו די רעכטע זייט פון דער גאס ווייל מיין שוועסטער דארף
קומען צוריק היינט נאכמיטאג

I see the sun in the morning from the kitchen
E'ech zeh di zin in der frieh fin di kich
איך זע די זון אין דער פרי פון די קיך

The house is on the right end of the street
Di hoyz iz aoyf di rekht suf fun di gas
די הויז איז אויף די רעכטע זייט פון די גאס

To wish - Tsu vintshen צו ווינטשן
Bad – Shlecht שלעכט
To get - Tsu bakumen צו באקומען
To forget - Tsu fargesen צו פארגעסן
Everybody / Everyone - Yederin יעדערן
Everybody / Everyone - Alemen אלעמען
Although – Chotsh כאטש
To feel - Tsu filn צו פילן
Great – Groys גרויס
To like - Tsu glaichen צו גלייכן
In front – Forent אין פארענט
Past – Fargangenhayt פארגאאנגענהייט

I don't want to wish anything bad
E'ech vil nisht vintshn epes shlecht
איך וויל נישט ווינטשן עפעס שלעכטס

I must forget everybody from my past.
ikh muz fargesn alemen fun meyn fargangenheyt.
איך מוז פארגעסן אלעמען פון מיין פארגאאנגגענהייט.

To feel well I must take vitamins
tsu filn gezunt muz ikh nemen vitamins
צו פילן געזונט מוז איך נעמען וויטאמינס

I am next to the person behind you
E'ech bin noent tsu di mentsh hinter dir
איך בין נאנט צו די מענטש הינטער דיר

There is a person in front of me
Es iz duh a mentsh in forent fin mir
עס איז דא א מענטש אין פארענט פון מיר

I go into the house from the front entrance and not through the yard.
ikh gey areyn in hoyz fun di fodishten arayngang un nisht durkh di hoyf.
איך גיי אריין אין הויז פון די פֿאָדישטען ארייַנגאאנג און נישט דורך די הויף.

Next (following, after) – Vayter ווייטער
Next (near, close) – Nuent נאָנט
Behind – Hinter הינטער
Well (as in doing well) – Gutt גוט
Restaurant – Restoran רעסטאראן
Bathroom – Klozet קלאָזעט
Goodbye (be well) – Zai gezunt זיי געזונט

Goodbye my friend.
zay gezunt meyn fraynd.
זייַ געזונט מייַן פרייַנד.

Which is the best restaurant in the area?
vos iz der bester restoran in der gegnt?
וואָס איז דער בעסטער רעסטאָראַן אין דער געגנט?

I can feel the heat.
ikh ken filn di hits.
איך קען פילן די היץ.

I need to repair a part of the cabinet of the bathroom.
ikh darf farikhtn a teyl fun di kabinet fun di klozet.
איך דאַרף פאַריכטן אַ טייל פון די קאַבינעט פון די קלאָזעט.

I want a car before next year
ikh vil a mashin fahr dem kummendiker yor
איך וויל אַ מאַשין פאַר דעם קומענדיקער יאר

I like the house, but it is very small.
ikh hob lib dem hoyz, ober es iz zeyer kleyn.
איך האָב ליב דעם הויז, אָבער עס איז זייער קליין.

*"Bathroom" is *klozet*. (It can mean "closet" as well.)

Please - Bit'e ביטע
To remove / to take out - Tsu nemen aroys צו נעמען ארויס
Beautiful – Sheyn שיין
To lift - Tsu heyben צו הייבן
Include / Including – Einshlissen איינשליסן
Belong – Geheren געהארן
To check - Tsu kontrolirn צו קאנטראלירן
Small – Kleyn קליין

She wants to remove this door, please
Zi vil aveknemen dem ti'er, bit'e
זי וויל אוועקנעמען דעם טיר, ביטע

We need to check the size of the house
Mir darfen kontrolirn di greys foon der hoyz
מיר דארפן קאנטראלירן די גרויס פון דער הויז

I want to lift this.
ikh vil das aoyfheybn.
איך וויל דאס אויפהייבן.

Can you please put the wood in the fire?
kent ir bite shteln di holts in di fayer?
קענט איר ביטע שטעלן די הָאלץ אין די פייַער?

This doesn't belong here, I need to check again
Duce gehert nisht do, e'ech darf vider kontrolirn
דאס געהערט נישט דא, איך דארף ווידער קאנטראלירן

Where is the synagogue?
Vu iz der shul
ווּ איז דער שול

*With the knowledge you've gained so far, now try to create your own sentences!

Real - Praktish פּראקטיש
Real - Faktish פאקטיש
Weather – Veter וועטער
Size – Groys גרויס
High – Hoych הויך
Doesn't – Nisht נישט
So – Azoy אזוי
Price – Prayz פרייז
To hold - Tsu halten צו האלטן
Hospital - Shpitol שפּיטאָל
Expensive – Tayer טייער

Is that a real diamond?
iz dos an emese diamant?
איז דאָס אַן אמתע דיאמענט?

This week the weather was very beautiful
Diy voch di veter iz geven zeyer sheyn
די וואך די וועטער איז געווען זייער שיין

I can pay this although the price is expensive
E'ech ken batsoln duce chotsh der prayz iz tayer
איך קען דאָס באַצאָלן כאטש דער פרייז איז טייער

Can you please hold my hand?
Kenstu bite haltn meyn hant?
קענצו ביטע האַלטן מיין האַנט?

Where is the hospital?
Vau iz der shpitol?
וואו איז דער שפּיטאָל?

The sun is high in the sky.
di zun iz hoykh in himl.
די זון איז הויך אין הימל.

Building Bridges

In Building Bridges, we take six conjugated verbs that have been selected after studies I have conducted for several months in order to determine which verbs are most commonly conjugated, and which are then automatically followed by an infinitive verb. For example, once you know how to say, "I need," "I want," "I can," and "I like," you will be able to connect words and say almost anything you want more correctly and understandably. The following three pages contain these six conjugated verbs in first, second, third, fourth, and fifth person, as well as some sample sentences. Please master the entire program up until here prior to venturing onto this section.

I want - E'ech vil איך וויל / **I need** - E'ech darf איך דארף
I can - E'ech ken איך קען
I like - E'ech glach איך גלייך
I go - E'ech gey איך גיי
I have - E'ech hob איך האב
I must / I have to - E'ech mizz איך מיז

I want to go to my apartment
E'ech vil geyn tsu meyn voynung
איך וויל גיין צו מיין וואונונג

I can go with you to the bus station
E'ech ken geyn mit ir tsu di oytobus stantsye
איך קען גיין מיט דיר צו די אויטאבוס סטאנצִיע

I need to leave the museum.
ikh darf avek geyen fun der muzeum.
איך דארף אוועקגייען פֿון דער מוזייאום

I like to eat oranges.
ikh hob lib tsu esn marantsn.
איך האָב ליב צו עסן מאַראַנצן.

I am going to teach a class
E'ech ga'i lernen a klas
איך גיי לערנען אַ קלאָס

I have to speak to my teacher
E'ech mizz reden tsu meyn lerer
איך מיז רעדן צו מיין לערער

Please master *every* single page up until here prior to attempting the following two pages!

You want - Di vilst די ווילסט

Do you want? - Vilstu? ?ווילסטו

He wants - Er vil ער וויל

Does he want? - Vil er? ?וויל ער

She wants - Zi vil זי וויל

Does she want? - Tut zi velen? ?טוט זי וועלן

We want - Mir vilen מיר ווילן

Do we want? - Tu'en mir vilen? ?טוען מיר וועלן

They want - Zey vilen זיי ווילן

Do they want? - Tu'en zey velen? ?טוען זיי וועלן

You (plural) want – Ir vilt איר ווילט

Do you (plural) want? – Vilt ir? ?ווילט איר

You need - Ir darft איר דארפט

Do you need? - Darft ir? ?דארפט איר

He needs - Er darf ער דארף

Does he need? - Tut er darfen? ?טוט ער דארפן

She needs - Zi darf זי דארף

Does she need? - Tut zi darfen? ?טוט זי דארפן

They need - Zey darfen זיי דארפן

Do they need? - Tu'en zey darfen? ?טוען זיי דארפן

You (plural) need – Ir darft איר דארפט

You can - Ir kent איר קענט

Can you? - Kent ir? קענט איר?

He can - Er ken ער קען

Can he? - Ken er? קען ער?

She can Zi ken זי קען

Can she? - Ken zi? קען זי?

We can - Mir kenin מיר קענען

Can we? - Kenin mir? קענען מיר?

They can Zey kenin זיי קענען

Can they? - Kenin zey? קענען זיי?

You (plural) can – Ir kent איר קענט

You like - Di glaichst די גלייכסט

Do you like? - Glaichstu? גלייכסטו?

He likes Er glaicht ער גלייכט

Does he like? - Tut er glaichen? טוט ער גלייכן?

She likes - Zi glaicht זי גלייכט

Does she like? - Tut zi glaichen? טוט זי גלייכן?

We like - Mir glaichen מיר גלייכן

Do we like? - Tu'en mir glaichen? טוען מיר גלייכן?

They like - Zey glaichen זיי גלייכן

Do they like? - Tu'en zey glaichen? טוען זיי גלייכן?

You (plural) like – Ir glaicht איר גלייכט

You go - Di geyst די גייסט

Do you go? - Tistu geyn? טיסטו גיין?

He goes - Er geyt ער גייט

Does he go? - Tut er geyn? טוט ער גיין?

She goes - Zi geyt זי גייט

Does she go? - Tut zi geyn? טוט זי גיין?

We go - Mir geyen מיר גיין

Do we go? - Tu'en mir geyn? טוען מיר גיין?

They go - Zey geyn זיי גיין

Do they go? - Tu'en zey geyn? טוען זיי גיין?

You (plural) go – Ir geht איר גייט

You have - Di hostz די האסט

Do you have? - Tsi hostu? צו האסטו?

He has - Er hott ער האט

Does he have? - Tut er hobn? טוט ער האבן?

She has - Zi hott זי האט

Does she have? - Tut zi hobn? טוט זי האבן?

We have - Mir hobn מיר האבן

Do we have? - Tu'en mir hobn? טוען מיר האבן?

They have - Zey hobn זיי האבן

Do they have? - Tu'en zey hobn? טוען זיי האבן?

You (plural) have - Alle hoben אלע האבן

You (plural) have - Ir hott איר האט

Do you want to go?
Di vilst geyn?
?די ווילסט גיין

He wants to fly
Er vil fli'en
ער וויל פליען

We want to swim
Mir vilen shvimen
מיר ווילן שווימען

Do they want to run?
Tsu vilen zey loyfen?
?צו ווילן זיי לויפן

Do you need to clean?
Di darfst romen?
?די דארפסט רוימען

She needs to sing a song
Zi darf zingen a lid
זי דארף זינגען א ליד

We need to travel
Mir darfen arumtsuforn
מיר דארפן ארומצופארן

They don't need to fight
Zey darfen zich nisht tsukreygn
זיי דארפן זיך נישט צוקריגן

You (plural) need to save your money.
ir (plural) muzt shporn aier gelt.
איר מיזט שפארן אייער געלט

Can you hear me?
Di kenst mich hern?
?די קענסט מיך הערן

He can dance very well
Er ken tantsn zeyer gut
ער קען טאנצן זייער גוט

We can go out tonight
Mir kenen aroysgeyn haynt ba nacht
מיר קענען ארויסגיין היינט ביינאכט

During an emergency, firefighters can break down a door.
Fayerleshers kenen tsubrekhn a tir beshas a noytfal.
פייערלעשערס קענען צוברעכן אַ טיר בשעת אַ נויטפאַל

Do you like to eat here?
Ir glaicht tsu esn do?
איר גלייכט צו עסן דא?

He likes to spend time here
Er glaicht tsu farbrengen tseyt do
איר גלייכט צו פארברענגען צייט דא

We like to fix the house
Mir glaichen zu reparyeren dem shtyb
מיר גלייכן צו רעפּאַרירן דעם שטיב

They like to cook
Zey glaichen tsu kochen
זיי גלייכן צו קאכן

You (plural) like to play soccer.
ir (plural) hot lib tsu shpiln fusbol.
איר האָט ליב צו שפּילן פוסבאָל.

Do you go to the movies on weekends?
Geyt ir in kino sof vokh?
גייט איר אין קינאָ סוף וואך?

He goes fishing
Er geyt khapen fish
ער גייט כאפן פיש

We are going to see the moon
Mir gehen zen di levuna
מיר געען זען די לבנה

They go out to eat at a restaurant every day.
zey geyn esn in a restoran yeden tog.
זיי גייןן עסן אין אַ רעסטאָראַן יעדן טאָג

Do you have money?
Tsi hott ir gelt?
צו האט איר געלט?

He needs to go to sleep
Er darf geyn shlofn
ער דארף גיין שלאפן

She must look outside
Zi mizz kiken aroys
זי מוז קיקן ארויס

We must sign our names
Mir mizzen shrayben unzer nemen
מיר מוזן שרייבן אונזער נעמען

They must send the letter
Zey mizzen shikn dem briv
זיי מוזן שיקן דעם בריוו

You (plural) have to stand in line.
ir (plural) muzt shteyn in a rey.
איר מוזט שטיין אין א ריי

Other Useful Tools in the Yiddish Language

Months - Chodoshim חדשים
January – Yanuar יאַנואַר
February – Februar פֿעברואַר
March – Marts מאַרץ
April – April אַפּריל
May – May מײַ
June – Yuni יוני
July – Yuli יולי
August – Oygust אויגוסט
September – September סעפּטעמבער
October – Oktober אָקטאָבער
November – November נאָוועמבער
December – Detsember דעצעמבער

Directions – Instruktsyes אינסטרוקציעס
North – Tsofn צפֿון
South – Darum דרום
East – Mizrach מזרח
West – Mariv מעריב

Days of the Week - Teg foon der voch טעג פֿון דער וואָך
Sunday – Zuntik זונטיק
Monday – Montik מאָנטיק
Tuesday – Dinstig דינסטיק
Wednesday – Mitvoch מיטוואָך
Thursday – Donershtig דאָנערשטיק
Friday – Freytig פֿרײַטיק
Saturday – Shabes שבת

Seasons – Tseytn צײַטן
Spring - Friling פֿרילינג
Summer – Zumer זומער
Autumn – Harbst האַרבסט
Winter – Vinter ווינטער

Colors – Kolieren קאלירן
Black – Shvarts שווארץ
White - Veyse ווייס
Blue – Bloy בלאָ
Yellow – Gale געל
Green – Grin גרין
Orange – Marants מאַראַנץ
Purple – Lila לילאַ
Brown – Broyn ברוין
Pink - Roz ראָז

Numbers – Numern נומערן
One – Eyns איינס
Two – Tsvey צוויי
Three – Drey דרײַ
Four – Fir פיר
Five – ind פינף
Six – Zeks זעקס
Seven – Zibn זיבן
Eight – Acht אכט
Nine – Neyn נײַן
Ten – Tsen צען
Twenty – Tsvantsik צוואַנציק
Thirty – Draysik דרײַסיק
Forty – Fertsik פערציק
Fifty – Fuftsik פופציק
Sixty – Zekhtsik זעכציק
Seventy – Zibetsik זיבעציק
Eighty – Akhtsik אַכציק
Ninety – Nayntsik נײַנציק
Hundred – Hundert הונדערט
Thousand – Toyznt טויזנט
Million – Milyon מיליאָן

Conclusion

Congratulations! You have completed all the tools needed to master the Yiddish language, and I hope that this has been a valuable learning experience. Now you have sufficient communication skills to be confident enough to embark on a visit to Brooklyn or Jerusalem, impress your friends, and boost your resume so *good luck*.

This program is available in other languages as well, and it is my fervent hope that my language learning programs will be used for good, enabling people from all corners of the globe and from all cultures and religions to be able to communicate harmoniously. After memorizing the required three hundred and fifty words, please perform a daily five-minute exercise by creating sentences in your head using these words. This simple exercise will help you grasp conversational communications even more effectively. Also, once you memorize the vocabulary on each page, follow it by using a notecard to cover the words you have just memorized and test yourself and follow *that* by going back and using this same notecard technique on the pages you studied during the previous days. This repetition technique will assist you in mastering these words in order to provide you with the tools to create your own sentences.

Every day, use this notecard technique on the words that you have just studied.

Everything in life has a catch. The catch here is just consistency. If you just open the book, and after the first few pages of studying the program, you put it down, then you will not gain anything. However, if you consistently dedicate a half hour daily to studying, as well as reviewing what you have learned from previous days, then you will quickly realize why this method is the most effective technique ever created to become conversational in a foreign language. My technique works! For anyone who doubts this technique, all I can say is that it has worked for me and hundreds of others.

Conversational
Yiddish
Quick and Easy
The Most Innovative Technique
to Learn the Yiddish Language

Part II

YATIR NITZANY

Introduction to the Program

In the first book, you were taught the 350 most useful words in the Yiddish language, which, once memorized, could be combined in order for you to create your own sentences. Now, with the knowledge you have gained, you can use those words in Conversational Yiddish Quick and Easy Part 2 and Part 3, in order to supplement the 350 words that you've already memorized. This combination of words and sentences will help you master the language to even greater proficiency and quicker than with other courses.

The books that comprise Parts 2 and 3 have progressed from just vocabulary and are now split into various categories that are useful in our everyday lives. These categories range from travel to food to school and work, and other similarly broad subjects. In contrast to various other methods, the topics that are covered also contain parts of vocabulary that are not often broached, such as the military, politics, and religion. With these more unusual topics for learning conversational languages, the student can learn quicker and easier. This method is flawless and it has proven itself time and time again.

If you decide to travel to the Brooklyn, then this book will help you speak the Yiddish language.

This method has worked for me and thousands of others. It surpasses any other language-learning method system currently on the market today.

This book, Part 2, specifically deals with practical aspects concerning travel, camping, transportation, city living, entertainment such as films, food including vegetables and fruit, shopping, family including grandparents, in-laws, and stepchildren, human anatomy, health, emergencies, and natural disasters, and home situations.

The sentences within each category can help you get by in other countries.

In relation to travel, for example, you are given sentences about food, airport necessities such as immigration, and passports. Helpful phrases include, "Where is the immigration and passport control inside the airport?" and "I want to order a bowl of cereal and toast with jelly." For flights there are informative combinations such as, "There is a long line of passengers in the terminal because of the delay on the runway." When arriving in another country options for what to say include, "We want to hire a driver for the tour. However, we want to pay with a credit card instead of cash" and, "On which street is the car-rental agency?

When discussing entertainment in another country and in a new language, you are provided with sentences and vocabulary that will help you interact with others. You can discuss art galleries and watching foreign films. For example, you may need to say to friends, "I need subtitles if I watch a foreign film" and, 'The mystery-suspense genre films are usually good movies'. You can talk about your own filming experience in front of the camera.

The selection of topics in this book is much wider than in ordinary courses. By including social issue such as incarceration, it will help you to engage with more people who speak the language you are learning.

Part 3 will deal with vocabulary and sentences relevant to indoor matters such as school and the office, but also a variety of professions and sports.

TRAVEL - REYZE עררז

Flight - fli פלי
Airplane - aeroplan ערָאָפּלאַן
Airport – flifeld פליפעלד
Terminal- luftvokzal לופֿטוואָקזאַל
Passport - pasport פּאַספּאָרט
Customs - tsolamt צאָלאַמט
Take off (airplane) – opflien אַפּפֿליִען
Landing - landing לאַנדינג
Departure - opfor אָפּפֿאָר
Arrival – ankum אנקום
Gate - toyer טוייער

I enjoy traveling.
ikh hob hnah fun travaling.
איך האָב הנאה פֿון טראַוואַלינג.

This is a very expensive flight.
dos iz a zeyer tayere fli.
דאָס איז אַ זייער טיַיערע פֿלי.

The airplane takes off in the morning and lands at night.
der eroplan heybt zikh an inderfri aun landt beynakht.
דער ערָאָפּלאַן הייבט זיך אן אינדערפֿרי און לאָנדעט ביַינאַכט.

We need to go to the departure gate instead of the arrival gate.
mir darfn geyn in di opfor toyer anshtot fun di onkumen toyer.
מיר דאַרפֿן גייין אין די אָפּפֿאָר טוייער אַנשטאָט פֿון די אָנקומען טוייער.

What is your final destination?
vos iz deyn letste destinatsie?
וואָס איז דיַין לעצטע דעסטינאַצייע?

The flight takes off at 3pm, but the boarding commences at 2:20pm.
di fli flit opavek 3:00, ober di bording heybt zikh on 14:20.
די פֿלי פֿליט אָפּ 3:00, אָבער די באָרדינג הייבט זיך אָן 14:20.

Luggage - bagazh באגאזש
Suitcase - tshemodan טשעמאָדאַן
Baggage claim - bagazh opnem באַאַזש אָפּנעם
Passenger – pasazhir פּאַסאַזשיר
Final Destination – letste destinatsie לעצטע דעסטינאַציע
Boarding - boarding באָרדינג
Runway - startpas סטאַרטפּאַס
Line – rey ריי
Delay - farhaltn פֿאַרהאַלטן
Wing - fligl פֿליגל

My suitcase is at the baggage claim.
meyn tshemodan iz bey di bagazh fodern.
מיין טשעמאָדאַן איז ביי די באַאַזש פֿאָדערן.

I am almost finished at customs.
ikh bin kmet fartik baym tsolamnt.
איך בין כמעט פֿאַרטיק ביַים צאָלאַמנט.

I don't like to sit above the wing of the airplane.
ikh hob nisht lib tsu zitsn ibern fligl funem eraflan.
איך האָב נישט ליב צו זיצן איבערן פֿליגל פֿונעם עראַפלאַן.

There is a long line of passengers in the terminal because of the delay on the runway.
es iz a lange rey fun pasajerz in di vokzal tsulib di farhaltung aoyf di startpas.
עס איז אַ לאַנגע ריי פֿון פּאַסאַזשערן אין די וואָקזאַל צוליב די פֿאַרהאַלטונג אויף די סטאַרטפּאַס.

Where is the passport control inside the airport?
vu iz di pas kontrol in di flifeld?
ווו איז די פּאַס קאָנטראָל אין די פֿליפֿעלד?

International flight – internatsyonale fli אינטערנאַציאָנאַלע פֿלי
Domestic flight – diner fli דינער פֿלי
Business class – biznes klas ביזנעס קלאַס
First class – ershter klas ערשטער קלאַס
Economy class – ekanamye klas עקאָנאָמיע קלאַס
Round trip - arum reyze אַרום רייזע
Direct flight - direkte fli דירעקטע פֿלי
One-way flight - eyn-veg fli איין-וועג פֿלי
Return flight - tsurikkumen fli צוריקקומען פֿלי
Flight attendant - fli-badiner פֿלי-באַדינער
Layover - aoysleyg אויסלייג
Connection - kesher קשר
Reservation - rezerveyshan רעזערוויישאָן

For international flights, you must be at the airport at least three hours before the flight.
far internatsyonale fleyts, ir muzt zeyn bay di aeroport bay mindster drey shoh eyder di fli.
פֿאַר אינטערנאַציאָנאַלע פֿלייטס, איר מוזט זיין ביי די אַעראָפֿאָרט ביי מינדסטער דריי שעה איידער די פֿלי.

For a domestic flight, I need to arrive at the airport at least two hours before the flight.
far a diner fli, ikh darf onkumen bay di aeroport bay mindster tsvey sheh eyder di fli.
פֿאַר אַ דינער פֿלי, איך דאַרף אָנקומען ביי די אַעראָפֿאָרט ביי מינדסטער צווי שעה איידער די פֿלי.

Business class is usually cheaper than first class.
biznes klas iz geveyntlekh mer bilik vi ershter klas.
ביזנעס קלאַס איז געוויינטלעך מער ביליק ווי ערשטע קלאַס.

A one-way ticket is cheaper than the round-trip ticket at the travel agency.
a eyn-veg bilet iz mer bilik vi der arum-reyze bilet bey der reyze agentur.
אַן איין-וועג בילעט איז מער ביליק ווי דער אַרום-רייזע בילעט ביי דער רייזע אַגענטור.

Security check – zikherheyt tshek זיכערהייט טשעק
Checked bags - opgeshtelt bagazh אָפּגעשטעלט באגאזש
Carry on bag - firn aoyf zekl פירן אויף זעקל
Business trip - biznes reyze ביזנעס רייזע
Check in counter – tshek in tombank טשעק אין טאָמבאַנק
Travel agency - reyze agentur רייזע אַגענטור
Visa - vize וויזע
Temporary visa – tseytveylige vize צייטווייליגע וויזע
Permanent visa – shtendik vize שטענדיק וויזע
Country – land לאַנד

I prefer a direct flight without a layover.
Ikh volt beser gevolt a direkt fli on a leyovuer.
איך וואָלט בעסער געוואָלט אַ דירעקט פלי אָן אַ לייאָווער.

I must reserve my return flight.
ikh muz rezervirn meyn tsurik fli.
איך מוז רעזערווירן מיין צוריק פלי.

Why do I need to remove my shoes at the security check?
Farvoz muz ikh oys ton mayne shikh baym zikherhayt tshek?
פֿאַרוואָס מוז איך אויסטאָן מײַנע שיך בײַם זיכערהײַט טשעק

I have three checked bags and one carry-on.
ikh hob dray opgeshtelt bagazh aun eyn firn-oyf.
איך האָב דרײַ אָפּגעשטעלט באַגאזש און איין פירן-אויף.

I have to ask my travel agent if this country requires a visa.
ikh muz fregn meyn reyze agent oyb dos land fodert a vize.
איך מוז פרעגן מיין רייזע אַגענט אויב דאָס לאַנד פאדערט אַ וויזע

The flight attendant told me to go to the check in counter.
di fli bagleyter dertseylt mir tsu geyn tsu di tshek in tombank.
די פלי באַגלייטער דערצײלט מיר צו גיין צו די טשעק אין טאָמבאַנק.

Trip – rayze רייַזע
Tourist - turist טוריסט
Tourism - turizm טוריזם
Holiday – vakatsie וואַקאַציע
Vacations - vakatsyes וואַקאַציעס
Currency exchange - krantkayt vexl קראַנטקייַט וועקסל
Port of entry - port fun pozitsye פּאָרט פון פּאָזיציע
Car rental agency – oyto dingeray אויטאָ דינגערייַ
Identification - identifikatsye אידענטיפיקאַציע
GPS - GPS גפּס
Road - veg וועג
Map - mape מאַפּע

I had an amazing trip.
ikh hob gehat aza sheyne rayze
איך האָב געהאַט אזאַ שיינע רייַזע

The currency exchange counter is past the port of entry.
di krantkayt vexl tombank iz noch di port fun pozitsye.
די קראַנטקייַט וועקסל טאָמבאַנק איז נאָך די פּאָרט פון פּאָזיציע.

There is a lot of tourism during the holidays and vacations.
es iz a plats fun turizm beshas di holidays aun vakatsye.
עס איז אַ פּלאַץ פון טוריזם בשעת די חגים און וואַקאַציעס

Where is the car-rental agency?
vu iz di oyto dingeray?
ווו איז די אויטאָ דינגערייַ?

You need to show your identification.
ir darfn tsu vayzn deyn legitimatsye.
איר דאַרפט ווייַזן די לעגיטימאַציע.

It's more convenient to use the GPS on the roads instead of a map.
es iz mer bakvem tsu nutsn di gps aoyf di roudz anshtot fun a mape.
עס איז מער באַקוועם צו נוצן די גפּס אויף די וועגן אַנשטאָט פון אַ מאַפּע.

Information center - informatsye tsenter אינפֿאָרמאַציע צענטער
Bank - Bank באַנק
Hotel – hatel האָטעל
Motel - motel מאָטעל
Hostel - hostel האָסטעל
Leisure - fraye tsayt פֿרייַע צייַט
Driver – firer פֿירער
Credit - Kredit קרעדיט
Cash - gelt געלט
A guide - a firer אַ פֿירער
Tour - rayze רייַזע
Ski resort - narte rizort נאַרטע ריזאָרט

Why is the information center closed today?
farvas iz der infarmatsye tsenter heynt farmakht?
פֿאַרוואָס איז דער אינפֿאַרמאַציע צענטער הייַנט פֿארמאכט?

When I am in a foreign country, I go to the bank before I go to the hotel.
ven ikh bin in a fremd land, ikh geyn tsu di bank eyder ikh geyn tsu di hotel.
ווען איך בין אין אַ פֿרעמד לאַנד, איך גיי צו די באַנק איידער איך גיי צו די האָטעל.

I need to book my leisure vacation at the ski resort today.
ikh darf bashtelen meyn fraye tsayt vakatsye in di narte rizort haynt.
איך דאַרף באַשטעלן מיין פֿרייַע צייַט וואַקאַציע אין די נאַרטע ריזאָרט הייַנט.

We want to hire a driver for the tour.
mir viln dingen a shofer far di rayze.
מיר ווילן דינגען אַ שאָפֿער פֿאַר די רייַזע.

We want to pay with a credit card instead of cash.
mir viln tsu tsoln mit a kredit kartl anshtot fun gelt.
מיר ווילן צאָלן מיט אַ קרעדיט קאַרטל אַנשטאָט פֿון געלט.

Does the tour include an English-speaking guide?
tut der rayze araynnemen an english-geredt firer?
טוט דער רייַזע אַרייַננעמען אַן ענגליש-גערעדט פֿירער?

TRANSPORTATION - TRANSPORTATYON טראַנספּאַרטאַטיאָן

Car - oyto אויטאָ
Train - ban באַן
Train station - ban stantsye באַן סטאַנציע
Train tracks - ban trax באַן טראַקס
Train cart - ban vogn באַן וואָגן
Taxi - Taxi טאַקסי
Subway - unterban אונטערבאַן
Station - stantsye סטאַנציע

Where is the public transportation?
vu iz der tsibur transperteyshan?
וואו איז דער ציבור טראַנספּערטיישאַן?

Where can I buy a bus ticket?
vu ken ikh koyfn a oytobus bilet?
וואו קען איך קויפן אַ אויטאָבוס בילעט?

Please call a taxi.
bite ruf a taxi.
ביטע רוף אַ טאַקסי.

In some cities, you don't need a car because you can rely on the subway.
in etlekhe shtet, ir ton nit darfn a mashin vayl ir kenen farlozn zikh di unterban.
אין עטלעכע שטעט, דארפט איר נישט אַ מאַשין ווייַל איר קענט פאַרלאָזן זיך אויף די אונטערבאַ

Where is the train station?
vu iz di ban stantsye?
וואו איז די באַן סטאַנציע?

The train cart is still stuck on the tracks.
der ban vogn iz nokh alts shtekn aoyf di shines.
דער באַן וואָגן איז נאָך אַלץ שטעקן אויף די שינעס.

Helicopter - helikopter העליקאָפּטער
Bus - oytobus אויטאָבוס
School bus – shule oytobus שולע אויטאָבוס
Limousine - limazin לימאַזין
Driver license - dreyver derloybenish דרייווער דערלויבעניש
Vehicle registration - formitl registratsye פאָרמיטל רעגיסטראַציע
License plate - derloybenish teler דערלויבעניש טעלער
Ticket - bilet בילעט
Ticket (penalty) - shtraf שטראָף
Motorcycle - mototsikl מאָטאָציקל
Scooter - skuter סקוטער

The motorcycles make loud noises.
di matarsiklen makhn hoykh kulus.
די מאָטאָרסיקלען מאכן הויך קולות.

Where can I rent a scooter?
vu ken ikh dingen a skuter?
ווו קען איך דינגען אַ סקוטער?

I want to plan a helicopter tour.
ikh viln tsu plan a helikopter rayze.
איך וויל פּלאַנען אַ העליקאָפּטער רייזע.

I want to go to the party in a limousine.
ikh viln geyn tsu der partey in a limazin.
איך וויל גיין צו דער פּאַרטיי אין אַ לימאַזין.

Don't forget to bring your driver's license and registration.
du zalst nisht fargesn tsu brengen deyn dreyver derloybenish aun registratsye.
דו זאלסט נישט פאַרגעסן צו ברענגען דיין דרייווער דערלויבעניש און רעגיסטראַציע.

The cop gave me a ticket because my license plate has expired.
der falitsey hat mir gegebn a bilet veyl meyn leysens teler iz aoysgegangen.
דער פאָליציי האט מיר געגעבן אַ בילעט ווייל מיין לייסענס טעלער איז אויסגעגאַנגען.

Truck – trok טראָק
Pickup truck - pikap trok פּיקאַפּ טראָק
Bicycle – velosiped װעלאָסיפּעד
Van - Van װאַן
Gas station – gaz stantsye גאַז סטאַנציע
Gasoline - gazolin גאַזאָלין
Tire – rayf רייַף
Oil change – oil toyshn אָיל טױשן
Tire change – toyshn di rayf טױשן די רייַף
Mechanic – mekhaniker מעכאַניקער

I can put my bicycle in my truck.
ikh ken shteln meyn velosiped in meyn trok.
איך קען שטעלן מײן װעלאָסיפּעד אין מײן טראָק.

Where is the gas station?
vu iz di gaz stantsye?
ווּ איז די גאַז סטאַנציע?

I need gasoline and also to put air in my tires.
ikh darf gazolin aun aoykh shteln luft in mayne rayfes.
איך דאַרף גאַזאָלין און אױך שטעלן לופט אין מײַנע רייפעס.

I need to take my car to the mechanic for a tire and oil change.
ikh darf tsu nemen meyn mashin tsu di mekhaniker far a rayf aun eyl toyshn.
איך דאַרף נעמען מײן מאַשין צו די מעכאַניקער פֿאַר אַ רייַף און אייל טױשן.

I can put my canoe in the van.
ikh ken shteln meyn kanu in di van.
איך קען שטעלן מײן קאַנו אין די װאַן.

Can I bring my yacht to the boat show at the marina?
ken ikh brengen meyn yakht tsu di shifl oysshtelung in der marina?
קען איך ברענגען מײן יאַכט צו די שיפל אױסשטעלונג אין דער מאַרינאַ?

Canoe - kanu קאַנו
Ship - shif שיף
Boat – shifl שיפל
Yacht - yakht יאַכט
Sailboat - zeglshifl זעגלשיפל
Motorboat - motorboat מאָטאָרבאָט
Marina - Marina מאַרינאַ
The dock - di dok די דאָק
Cruise - kruz קרוז
Cruise ship - arumforn shif אַרומפאָרן שיף
Ferry - feri פערי
Submarine - submarin סובמאַרין

I prefer a motorboat instead of a sailboat.
ikh volt beser gevolt a motorshifl anshtot fun a zeglshifl.
איך וואָלט בעסער געוואָלט אַ מאָטאָרשיפל אנשטאָט פון אַ זעגלשיפל.

I want to leave my boat at the dock on the island.
ikh vil lozn meyn shifl bay di dok aoyf dem inzl.
איך וויל לאָזן מיין שיפל ביי די דאָק אויף דעם אינזל.

This spot is a popular stopping point for the cruise ship.
dem ort iz a populere stopping punkt far di arumforn shif.
דעם אָרט איז אַ פאָפּולערע סטאָפּפינג פונקט פאַר די אַרומפאָרן שיף.

This was an excellent cruise.
dos iz geven a oysgetseykhnt arumforn.
דאָס איז געוועןָ אַ אויסגעצייכנט אַרומפאָרן.

Do you have the schedule for the ferry?
Hot ir di plan far di prom?
האָט איר די פּלאַן פאַר די פּראָם?

The submarine is yellow.
di submarin iz gel.
די סובמאַרין איז געל.

CITY - SHTOT שטאָט

Town - Shtot שטאָט
Village - Dorf דאָרף
House - Hoyz הויז
Home – Heym היים
Apartment – dirah דירה
Building - binyin בנין
Highrise – hoykher binyin הויכער בנין
Tower - turem טורעם
Neighborhood – gegent געגענט

Is this a city or a village?
Iz dos a shtot oder a dorf?
?איז דאָס אַ שטאָט אָדער אַ דאָרף

Does he live in a house or an apartment?
Voynt er in a hoyz oder a dirah?
?וווינט ער אין אַ הויז אדער אַ דירה

This residential building does not have an elevator, just stairs.
Dem rezidentshal binyin hat nisht a lift, nor trep.
.דעם רעזידענטשאַל בנין האט נישט אַ ליפט, נאָר טרעפ

These high-rise buildings are located in the center city.
di hoykhe binyinim zenen in di tsenter fun shtot.
.די הויכע בנינים זענען אין די צענטער פון שטאָט

The tower is tall but the building beside it is very short.
Der turem iz hoykh ober der binyin lebn im iz zeyer kurts.
.דער טורעם איז הויך אָבער דער בנין לעבן אים איז זייער קורץ

This is a beautiful neighborhood.
Dos iz a sheyne gegnt.
.דאָס איז אַ שיינע געגנט

There is a fence around the construction site.
Es iz a ployt arum di kanstrakshan plats.
.עס איז אַ פלויט אַרום די קאָנסטראַקשאַן פּלאַץ

72

Office building – byuro binyin ביורָא בנין

Post office – postamt פָּאסטאמט

Location - ort אָרט

Elevator – lift ליפט

Stairs - trep טרעפ

Fence - ployt פלויט

Construction site – kanstrakshan plats קאָנסטראָקשאָן פלאַץ

Bridge - brik בריק

Gate - toyer טויער

City hall – shtot zal שטאָט זאַל

Mayor - birgermayster בירגערמײַסטער

Fire department – feyer apteylung פייער אפטיילונג

Pedestrians - padestryanz פּאַדעסטריאַנז

Crosswalk - krosvok קראָסוואָק

The post office is located in that office building.
Di post byuro iz in dem ofis binyin.
די פּאָסט ביורָא איז אין דעם אָפיס בנין.

The bridge is closed today.
Di brik iz heynt farmakht.
די בריק איז היינט פארמאכט.

The gate is open.
Der toyer iz ofn.
דער טויער איז אָפן.

The fire department is located in the building next to city hall.
Di feyer department gefint zikh in dem gebeyde nebn shtat zal.
די פייער דעפארטמענט געפינט זיך אין דעם געביידע נעבן שטאט זאַל.

The mayor of Brooklyn is very well known.
Der birgermeyster fun bruklin iz zeyer bakant.
דער בירגערמייסטער פון ברוקלין איז זייער באקאנט.

The pedestrians use the crosswalk to cross the road.
di fusgeyer nitsn di krossvok tsu geyn ariber de veg.
די פוסגייער ניצן די קראָססוואָק צו גיין אריבער די וועג

Street - gass גאַס
Main street - hoypt gass הויפט גאַס
To park - tsu parkirn צו פּאַרקירן
Parking lot - parkirplats פּאַרקירפּלאַץ
Sidewalk - trotuar טראָטוואַר
Traffic - farker פֿאַרקער
Traffic light - farker likht פֿאַרקער ליכט
Red light – royte likht רויטע ליכט
Yellow light – gele likht געלע ליכט
Green light – grine likht גרינע ליכט

Parking is on the main street and not on the sidewalk.
parking iz oyf di hoypt gas un nisht aoyf dem trotvar.
די פּאַרקינג איז אויף די הויפט גאַס און נישט אויף דעם טראָטוואַר.

Where is the parking lot?
vu iz der parkirplats?
ווו איז דער פּאַרקירפּלאַץ?

The traffic is very bad today.
der trafik iz heynt zeyer shlekht.
דער טראַפיק איז היינט זייער שלעכט.

You must avoid the fast lane because it's a toll lane.
ir muzt oysmeydn di shnel shteg vayl es iz an optsol shteg.
איר מוזט אויסמיידן די שנעל שטעג ווייַל עס איז אַן אָפּצאָל שטעג.

We don't like to drive on the highway.
mir hobn nisht lib tsu forn oyf der shosey.
מיר האָבן נישט ליב צו פאָרן אויף דער שאָסיי.

At a red light you need to stop, at a yellow light you must be prepared to stop and at a green you can drive.
bey a royt likht darf men apshteln, bey a gel likht darf men zikh greytn apshteln aun bey a grin ken men faren.
ביי אַ רויט ליכט דארף מען אפשטעלן, ביי אַ געל ליכט דארף מען זיך גרייַטן אפשטעלן און ביי אַ גרין קען מען פאָרן.

This road has too many traffic lights.
der veg hat tsu file farker leyts.
דער וועג האָט צו פיל פאַרקער ליכט.

Lane - leyn ליין
Toll lane - tol shteg טאָל שטעג
Fast lane – shnel leyn שנעל ליין
Slow lane – pamelekh shteg פּאַמעלעך שטעג
Right lane – rekht shteg רעכט שטעג
Left lane – links shteg לינקס שטעג
Highway – shosey שאָסיי
Intersection - intersekshan אינטערסעקשאַן
Tunnel – tunel טונעל
U-turn - u-drey ו-דריי
Shortcut - durkhveg דורכוועג
Bypass - beypas בייפּאַס
Stop sign – stopshild סטאָפּשילד

At the intersection, we need to stay in the left lane instead of the right lane because that's a bus lane.
in di intersekshan, mir darfn blaybn in di links shteg anshtot fun di rekht shteg vayl dos iz an otobus shteg.
אין די אינטערסעקשאַן, מיר דאַרפֿן בלייבן אין די לינקע שטעג אַנשטאָט פון די רעכטע שטעג ווייַל דאָס איז אַן אויטאָבוס שטעג.

The tunnel seems longer than yesterday.
der tunel zet oys lenger vi nekhtn.
דער טונעל זעט אויס לענגער ווי נעכטן.

It's a short drive.
es iz a kurtse for.
עס איז אַ קורצע פאָר.

The next bus stop is far away from here.
der kumedike oytobus haltn iz vayt avek fun do.
דער קומעדיקע אויטאָבוס האַלטן איז ווייַט אַוועק פון דאָ.

You need to turn right at the stop sign and then continue on straight.
ir darft dreyen rekht bay di haltn tseykhn aun dan forzetsn glaykh.
איר דאַרפֿט דרייען רעכטס בייַ די האַלטן צייכן און דאַן פאַרזעצן גלייַך.

Capital – hoyptshtot הויפּטשטאָט
Port - port פּאָרט
Road - veg וועג
Trail - shteg שטעג
Path – derekh דרך
Bus station - oytobus stantsye אויטאָבוס סטאַנציע
Bus stop – oytobus haltn אויטאָבוס האַלטן
Night club – nakht klub נאַכט קלוב
Downtown – untershtot אונטערשטאָט
District - distrikt דיסטריקט
County - kaunti קאאונטי
Statue - Statue סטאַטוע
Monument - denkmol דענקמאָל
Castle – shlos שלאָס

The capital is a major attraction point for tourists.
di hoyptshtot iz a hoypt atraktsiye punkt far turisten.
די הויפּטשטאָט איז אַ הויפּט אַטראַקציע פונקט פֿאַר טוריסטן

The hotel is next to the port.
der hotel iz lebn di port.
דער האָטעל איז לעבן די פּאָרט.

The nightclub is located in the downtown area.
der nakht klub iz in di untershtot gegnt.
דער נאַכט קלוב איז אין די אונטערשטאָט געגנט.

In which district do you live?
in velkhe distrikt voynt ir?
אין וועלכע דיסטריקט ווינט איר?

This statue is a city monument.
di statue iz a shtot denkmol.
די סטאַטוע איז אַ שטאָט דענקמאָל.

This is an ancient castle.
das iz an alte shlos.
דאַס איז אַן אַלטע שלאָס.

Church - kirkh קירך
Cathedral - katedral קאַטעדראַל
Synagogue – shul שול
Mosque - moskve מאָסקווע
Science museum – visnshaft muzey וויסנשאַפֿט מוזיי
Zoo – zugortn זוגאָרטן
Playground – shpilplats שפּילפּלאַץ
Swimming pool – shvimeray שווימעריַי
Jail / prison – tfisah תּפֿיסה

Where is the local church?
vu iz di hige kirkh?
ווּ איז די היגע קירך?

That is a beautiful cathedral.
dos iz a sheyne katidral.
דאָס איז אַ שיינע קאַטידראַל.

Do you want to go to the zoo or the science museum?
Vilt ir geyen in der zugortn oder visnshaft muzey?
ווילט איר גייען אין דער זוגאָרטן אָדער וויסנשאַפֿט מוזיי?

The children are in the playground.
di kinder zenen baym shpilplats.
די קינדער זענען ביַים שפּילפּלאַץ.

The swimming pool is closed for the community today.
di shvimeray iz farmakht far di khl haynt.
די שווימעריַי איז פֿאַרמאַכט פֿאַר די קהל היַינט.

You need to follow the trail alongside the main street to reach the bus station.
ir muzt nochgeyn di shteg vos geyt noch di hoypt gas tsu dergreykhn di otobus stantsye.
איר מוסט נאָכגיין די שטעג וואָס גייט נאָך די הויפֿט גאָס צו דערגרייכן די אויטאָבוס סטאַנצִיע.

There is a jail in this county.
es iz do a tfise in dem kounti.
עס איז דאָ אַ תּפֿיסה אין דעם קאָונטי.

ENTERTAINMENT - FARVAYLUNG פֿאַרווייַלונג

Film / movie - Film פֿילם
Theater (movie theater) - kino קינאָ
Actor - aktyor אַקטיאָר
Actress - aktrise אַקטריסע
Genre – zhaner זשאַנער
Subtitles – unterkeplen אונטערקעפּלן
Action film - kamf film קאַמף פֿילם
Foreign film - fremd film פֿרעמד פֿילם
Mystery film – misterye film מיסטעריע פֿילם
Suspense film – shpanung film שפּאַנונג פֿילם

There are three new movies at the theater that I want to see.
es zenen doh drey neye kinos in teater vos ikh vil zehen.
עס זענען דא דריי נייע קינאָס אין טעאַטער וואָס איך וויל זען.

He is a really good actor.
er iz take a guter aktyor.
ער איז טאַקע אַ גוטער אַקטיאָר.

She is an excellent actress
zi iz a oysgetseykhente aktrise
זי איז אַן אויסגעצייכנטע אַקטריסע

That was a good action movie
dos iz geven a gut kamf film
דאָס איז געווען אַ גוט קאַמף פֿילם

We need subtitles if we watch a foreign film.
mir darfn unterkepln oyb mir zen a fremd film.
מיר דאַרפֿן אונטערקעפּלן אויב מיר זען אַ פֿרעמדע פֿילם.

Mystery or suspense films are usually good movies.
misterye oder shpanung films zenen geventlech gute kinos.
מיסטעריע אָדער שפּאַנונג פֿילמס זענען געווענדליך גוטע קינאָס

Documentary film – dokumentar film פילם דאָקומענטאַר

Biographies - byografyes ביאָגראפיעס

Drama film - drame film פילם דראַמע

Comedy film - komedye film פילם קאָמעדיע

Romance film - romans film פילם ראָמאַנס

Horror film - groyl film פילם גרויל

Animation film – animirte film פילם אַנימירטע

Cartoon – kartine קאַרטינע

Director – direktor דירעקטאָר

Producer - produtsirer פּראָדוצירער

Audience/Crowd – oylem עולם

Sometimes biographies are boring to watch.
amul zaynen biografies nudne tsu kukn
אַמאָל זײַנען ביאַגראַפֿיעס נודנע צו קוקן.

I like to watch horror movies.
ikh hob lib tsu kukn oyf groyl filmn
איך האָב ליב צו קוקן אויף גרויל פֿילמן

It's fun to watch animated movies.
es iz a shpas tsu kukn oyf animated kino.
עס איזאַ שפּאַס צו קוקן אויף אַנימאַטעד קינאָ.

The director and the producer can meet the audience today.
der direktor aun der produtsirer kenen trefn dem oylem haynt.
דער דירעקטאָר און דער פּראָדוצירער קענען טרעפֿן דעם עולם היינט.

I like documentary films. However, comedy-drama or romance films are better.
ikh gleich dokiumenteri films. ober, komedye-drame oder romans films zenen beser.
איך גלייך דאַקומענטערי פֿילמס. אָבער, קאָמעדיע-דראַמע אָדער ראָמאַנס פֿילמס זענען בעסער.

Entertainment - farvaylung פֿאַרוויַילונג
Television - televizye טעלעוויזיע
A show (as in television) - program פּראָגראַם
A show (as in live performance) - forshtelung פֿאָרשטעלונג
Channel – Kanal קאַנאַל
Series (in television) - serye סעריע
Commercial – reklame רעקלאַמע
Episode - epizod עפּיזאָד
Script - shrift שריפֿט
Screen – ekran עקראַן
Camera - aparat אַפּאַראַט

It's time to buy a new television.
es iz tseyt tsu koyfn a naye televizye.
עס איז צייַט צו קויפֿן אַ ניַיע טעלעוויזיע.

This was the first episode of this television show, yet it was a long series.
dos iz geven der ershter epizod fun dem televizye program, ober es iz geven a lange serye.
דאָס איז געווען דער ערשטער עפּיזאָד פֿון דעם טעלעוויזיע פּראָגראַם, אָבער עס איז געווען אַ לאַנגע סעריע.

There aren't any commercials on this channel.
es iz keyn mol nisht do keyn reklames af dem kanal.
עס איז קיין מאָל נישט דאָ קיין רעקלאַמעס אויף דעם קאַנאַל

I must read my script in front of the screen and the camera
ikh muz leyenen meyn skript far dem ekran un fotoaparat
איך מוז לייענען מיין סקריפֿט פֿאַר דעם עקראַן און פֿאָטאָאַפּאַראַט

We want to enjoy the entertainment this evening.
mir viln hnah hobn fun di farvaylung dem ovnt.
מיר ווילן הנאה האָבן פֿון די פֿאַרוויַילונג דעם אָוונט.

News - neyes נייעס
News station – nayes stantsye נייַעס סטאַנציע
News reporter - nayes reporter נייַעס רעפּאָרטער
Screening - filmvayzung פֿילמװייַזונג
Live broadcast - leybn brodkast לעבן בראָדקאַסט
Broadcast - brodkast בראָדקאַסט
Headline – kopen shura - קאָפּן שורה
Viewer – tsukuker צוקוקער
Speech – Rede רעדע

This news reporter works for our local news station.
der nayes reporter arbet far undzer hige nayes stantsye.
דער נייַעס רעפּאָרטער אַרבעט פֿאַר אונדזער היגע נייַעס סטאַנציע.

They decided to screen a live broadcast on the news.
zey hobn bashlosn tsu vayzn a direkte brodkast af di nayes.
זיי האָבן באַשלאָסן צו װייַזן אַ דירעקטע בראָדקאַסט אױף די נייַעס

The news station featured the headlines before the program began.
di neyes stantsye hot aroysgeshtelt di kepel shiros eyder di program hot zikh ongehoybn.
די נייַעס סטאַנסיע האָט אַרױסגעלייגט די קאָפּן שורות איידער די פּראָגראַם האָט זיך אָנגעהױבן

Tonight, all the details about the incident were mentioned on the news.
heynt bay nakht zenen ale di protim vegn dem intsident geven dermant aoyf di nayes.
היינט ביי נאַכט זענען אַלע די פּרטים װעגן דעם אינסידענט געװען דערמאַנט אױף די נייַעס.

The viewers wanted to hear the presidential speech today.
di tsukukers hobn gevalt hern di prezidentlikhe rede heynt.
די צוקוקערס האָבן געװאָלט הערן די פּרעזידענטליכע רעדע היינט.

Theater (play) – teater טעאַטער
A musical - muzikalishe piese מוזעקאַלישע פּיעסע
A play - a piese א פּיעסע
Stage – bine בינע
Audition - adishan אַדישאַן
Performance – forshtelung פֿאָרשטעלונג
Box office – kase קאַסע
Ticket – bilet בילעט
Singer – (m) zinger זינגער, (f) zingerin זינגערין
Band – kapelie קאַפּעליִע
Orchestra - orkester אָרקעסטער
Opera - opera אָפּעראַ

It was a great musical performance.
es iz geven a mekhtike muzikalishe forshtelung.
עס איז געװען אַ מעכטיקע מוזיקאַלישע פֿאָרשטעלונג

Can I perform for the play on this stage?
ken ikh onshteln a piese oyf dem bine?
?קען איך אָנשטעלן אַ פּיעסע אױף דעם בינע

She is the lead singer of the band.
zi iz di hoypt zingerin inem kapelie.
זי איז די הױפּט זינגערין אינעם קאַפּעליִע.

I will go to the box office tomorrow to purchase tickets for the opera.
Morgin vel ikh geyen in kase tsu koyfn biletn far der opera
מאָרגן װעל איך גייען אין קאַסע צו קױפֿן בילעטן פֿאַר דער אָפּעראַ

The orchestra needs to perform below the stage.
der orkester darf shpiln unter der bine.
דער אָרקעסטער דאַרף שפּילן אונטער דער בינע.

Music - muzik מוזיק
Song - lid ליד
Musical instrument – muzikalishe instrument מוזיקאלישע אינסטרומענט
Drum - poyk פויק
Guitar - gitar גיטאַר
Piano - pyane פּיאַנע
Trumpet – trampet טראָמפּעט
Violin – fidl פֿידל
Flute - fleyt פֿלייט
Art - kunst קונסט
Gallery - galerye גאַלעריע
Studio - studyo סטודיאָ
Museum – muzey מוזיי

I like to listen to this type of music. I hope to hear a good song.
ikh hob lib tsu hern dem sort muzik. Ikh hof az ikh vel hern a sheyn lid.
איך האָב ליב צו הערן דעם סאָרט מוזיק. איך האָף אַז איך וועל הערן אַ שיין ליד.

The common musical instruments that are used in a concert are drums, guitars, pianos, trumpets, violins, and flutes.
di gevendliche muzikalishe instrumentn vos men shpilt in konsert zaynen poykn, gitars, pianos, trumpeytn, fidln, un fleytn.
די געוועדליכע מוזיקאַלישע אינסטרומענטן וואָז מען שפּילט אין קאָנסערטן זײַנען פּויקן, גיטאַרס, פּיאַנאָס, טרומפּייטן, פֿידלן, און פֿלייטן.

The art gallery has a studio for rent.
di kunst galerye hat a studye tsu fardingen.
די קונסט גאַלעריע האָט אַ סטודיע צו פֿאַרדינגען.

I went to an art museum yesterday.
ikh bin nekhtn gegangen in a kunst muzey.
איך בין נעכטן געגאַנגען אין אַ קונסט מוזיי.

FOOD - ESNVARG עסנווארג

Grocery store - shpayzkrom שפּײַזקראָם
Market - mark מאַרק
Supermarket - supermark סופּערמאַרק
Groceries – shpayzvarg i שפּײַזװאַרג
Butcher shop – katsev קצב
Butcher – katsev קצב
Bakery - bekeray בעקערײַ
Baker - beker בעקער
Breakfast – frishtik פֿרישטיק
Lunch – mitog מיטאָג
Dinner – vetshere װעטשערע
Meat - fleysh פֿלייש
Chicken - hindl הינדל
Seafood – yam frukht ים פֿרוכט

Where is the nearest grocery store?
vu iz di nenste shpayzkrom?
װוּ איז די נענסטע שפּײַזקראָם?

Where can I buy meat and chicken?
vu ken ikh koyfn fleysh un hindl?
װוּ קען איך קויפֿן פֿלייש און הינדל?

The butcher shop is near the bakery.
lebn der bekerey iz der ktsb.
לעבן דער בעקערײַ איז דער קצב.

I have to go to the market, to buy a half kilo of meat.
ikh darf geyn in mark, tsu koyfn a halb kilo fleysh.
איך דאַרף גיין אין מאַרק, צו קויפֿן אַ האַלב קילאָ פֿלייש.

The groceries are already in the car.
Dos shpayzvarg iz shoyn in oyto.
דאָס שפּײַזװאַרג איז שוין אין אויטאָ.

Egg – ey איי
Milk - milkh מילך
Butter – puter פּוטער
Cheese - kez קעז
Bread - broyt ברויט
Flour - mel מעל
Oil - boyml בוימל
Baked - gebakn געבאקן
Cake - kukhn קוכן
Beer - bir ביר
Wine – veyn וויין
Cinnamon - tsimering צימערינג
Powder - proshik פּראָשיק
Mustard - zeneft זענעפֿט

We need to buy flour, eggs, milk, butter, and oil to bake my cake.
mir darfn koyfn mel, eyer, milkh, puter aun boyml tsu bakn meyn kukhn.
מיר דארפֿן קויפֿן מעל, אייער, מילך, פּוטער און בוימל צו באַקן מיין קוכן.

For lunch, we can eat seafood, and pasta for dinner.
Af mitog, mir kenen esn yam frukht , un af vetshere.
אויף מיטאָג, מיר קענען עסן ים פֿרוכט, און אויף וועטשערע, לאָקשן

I usually eat bread with a slice of cheese for breakfast.
Ikh es geveyntlekh broyt mit a reftl kez af frishtik.
איך עס געוויינטלעך ברויט מיט א רעפֿטל קעז אויף פֿרישטיק.

I like ketchup and mustard on my hotdog.
ikh hob lib ketshup un zenef af mayn hotdog
איך האָב ליב קעטשופ און זענעפֿט אויף מײַן האָטדאָג

The rolls are covered with cinnamon.
di rolls zenen badekt mit tsimering.
די ראָלס זענען באדעקט מיט צימערינג.

We drink beer or wine during the meal.
mir trinken bir oder vayn beshas di moltsayt.
מיר טרינקען ביר אָדער וויין בשעת די מאָלצייַט.

85

Menu - meniu מעניו
Beef - rindfleysh רינדפֿלייש
Lamb - shepsnfleysh שעפּסנפֿלייש
Pork - khazerfleysh חזירפֿלייש
Steak - bifsteyk ביפסטייק
Hamburger - hamburger האַמבורגער
Water – vaser וואַסער
Salad - salat סאַלאַט
Soup - zup זופ
Appetizer – farshpayz פֿאַרשפּייַז
Entrée – hoyptmaykhl הויפּטמאַכל

Do you have a menu in English?
hot ir an englishe meniu
האָט איר אַן ענגלישע מעניו

Which is preferable, the fried fish or the grilled lamb?
vos iz bilkher, di gepreglt fish oder di grild shepsnfleysh?
?וועלכע איז בעסער, די געפרעגלטע פיש אָדער די גריליד שעפּסנפֿלייש

I want to order a cup of water, a soup for my appetizer, and pizza for my entrée.
ikh bashteln a glezel vaser, a zup far meyn farshpayz, aun pitse far meyn hoyptmaykhl.
איך וויל באַשטעלן אַ גלעזל וואַסער ,אַ זופ פֿאַר מייַן פֿאַרשפּייַז ,און פּיצע פֿאַר מייַן
הויפּטמאַכל.

I want to order a steak for myself, a hamburger for my son, and ice cream for my wife.
ikh vilbashteln a bifsteyk far zikh, a hamburger far meyn zun, aun eyz krem far meyn froy.
איך וויל באַשטעלן אַ ביפסטייק פֿאַר זיך ,אַ האַמבורגער פֿאַר מיין זון ,און אייז
קרעם פֿאַר מיין פֿרוי.

What type of dessert is included with my coffee?
vos far a min desertiz arayngerekhnt mit meyn kave?
?וואָס פֿאַר אַ מין דעסערט איז אַרייַנגערעכנט מיט מייַן קאַווע

86

Cooked - gekokht געקאָכט
Boiled - gekokht געקאָכט
Fried - gebratn געבראַטן
Broiled - broyld בּרוילד
Grilled - grild גרילד
Raw - roy רוי
Dessert – desert דעסערט
Ice cream - eyz krem אײז קרעם
Coffee – kave קאַװע
Tea – tey טײ
Olive oil – masline boyml מאַסלינע בוימל
Fish – fish פיש
Juice - zaft זאַפט
Honey - honik האָניק
Sugar - tsuker צוקער

Can I order a salad with a hardboiled egg and olive oil on the side?
kenikh bashteln a salat mit a harteey un masline boyml aoyf di zayt?
?קען איך באַשטעלן אַ סאַלאַט מיט אַ האַרטע אײַ און מאַסלינע בוימל אויף די זײַט

Is the piece of fish in the sushi cooked or raw?
iz di shtik fish in di sushi gekokht oder roy?
?איז די שטיק פיש אין די סושי געקאָכט אָדער רוי

I want to order a fruit juice instead of a soda.
ikh vil bashteln a frukht zaft anshtot a sode
איך װיל באַשטעלן אַ פרוכט זאַפט אַנשטאָט אַ סאָדע

I want to order tea with a teaspoon of honey instead of sugar.
ikh vil bashtelntey mit a lefele fun honik anshtot fun tsuker.
.איך װיל באַשטעלן טײ מיט אַ לעפעלע פון האָניק אַנשטאָט פון צוקער

The tip is 15% at this restaurant.
der trinkgelt iz 15% in dem restoran.
.דער טרינקגעלט איז 15% אין דעם רעסטאָראַן

Vegetarian - vegetaryer וועגעטאַריער
Vegan – Veganer וועגאַנער
Dairy - milkhik מילכיק
Dairy products - milkhike produktn מילכיקע פּראָדוקטן
Salt - zalts זאַלץ
Pepper - fefer פעפער
Flavor - tam טעם
Spices - gevirtsn געווירצן
Nuts - nislekh ניסלעך
Peanuts - stashkes סטאַשקעס

I don't eat meat because I am a vegetarian.
ikh es nisht keyn fleysh vayl ikh bin a vegetaryer.
.איך עס נישט קיין פלייש ווייל איך בין אַ וועגעטאַריער

My brother won't eat dairy products because he is a vegan.
mayn bruder vet nisht esn milkhike produktn vayl er iz a veganer.
.מיַין ברודער וועט נישט עסן מילכיקע פּראָדוקטן ווייל ער איז אַ וועגאַנער

Food tastes much better with salt, pepper, and other spices.
esnvarg shmekt fil beser mit zalts, fefer un andere gevirtsn.
.עסנוואַרג שמעקט פיל בעסער מיט זאַלץ, פעפער און אנדערע געווירצן

The only things I have in my freezer are popsicles.
Der eynsike zakh vos ikh hob in meyn frierke iz popsikles.
.דער איינסיקע זאַך וואָס איך האָב אין מיַין פֿריִערקע איז פּאָפּסיקעלס

No chocolate, candy, or whipped cream until after dinner.
Nisht keyn shokolad, zisvarg oder shlag biz nokh mitog.
.נישט קיין שאָקאָלאַד, זיסוואַרג אָדער שלאַג ביז נאָך מיטאָג

I want to try a sample of that piece of cheese.
ikh vil farzukhn a shtilk fun dem kez.
איך וויל פֿאַרזוכן אַ שטיקל פֿון דעם קעז

I have allergies to nuts and peanuts.
ikh bin alergish tsu nis un stashkes.
איך בין אַלערגיש צו ניס און סטאַשקעס

Sauce - sos סאָס
Sandwich - sendvitsh סענדוויטש
Mayonnaise - freyz מייאָנעז
Rice - rayz רייַז
Fries - fritlekh פֿריטלעך
Soy - soy סוי
Jelly - ayngemakhs איינגעמאַכס
Chocolate - shokolad שאָקאָלאַד
Cookie - kikhl קיכל
A candy - a tzukerl אַ צוקערל
Whipped cream – shlag שלאַג
Popsicle - popsikel פּאָפּסיקלע
Frozen - farfroyrn פֿאַרפֿרוירן
Thawed – tsetopet צעטאָפּעט

This sauce is delicious.
der sos iz geshmak.
דער סאָס איז געשמאַק.

Why do you always put mayonnaise on your sandwich?
farvos leygstu shtendik mayonez oyf dayne shnitkes?
פֿאַרוואָס לייגסטו שטענדיק מייאָנעז אויף דייַנע שניטקעס

The food is still frozen so we need to wait for it to thaw.
dos esn iz nokh alts farfroyrn iz mir muzn vartn az es zol zikh tsetopn.
דאָס עסן איז נאָך אַלץ פֿאַרפֿרוירן איז מיר מוזן ווארטן אַז עס זאָל זיך צעטאָפּן.

Please bring me a bowl of cereal and a slice of toasted bread with jelly.
bite brengt mir a shisl kashe un a reftl fun tostmit ayngemakhs.
ביטע ברענגט מיר אַ שיסל קאַשע און אַ רעפטל טאָסט מיט איינגעמאַכס.

It's healthier to eat rice than fries.
es iz mer gezunttsu esn rayz vi fritlekh.
עס איז מער געזונט צו עסן רייַז ווי פֿריטלעך.

VEGETABLES - GRINSN גרינסן

Tomato - pomidor פּאָמידאָר
Carrot - mer מער
Lettuce - shalatn שאַלאַטן
Radish - retekh רעטעך
Beet - burke בורקי
Chard - tshad טשאַד
Eggplant - patlezhan פּאַטלעזשאַן
Bell Pepper – zise fefer זיסע פֿעפֿער
Hot pepper – heyse fefer הייסע פֿעפּער

Grilled vegetables or steamed vegetables are popular side dishes at restaurants.
grilirte grinsn oder gedemfte grinsn zenen populere maykholim in restorantn. גרעלירטע גרינסן אָדער געדעמפֿטע גרינסן זענען פּאָפּולערע מאכלים אין רעסטראַנטן.

There are carrots, bell peppers, lettuce, and radishes in my salad.
do zaynen mern, zise fefers, shalatn, un retekher in mayn salat.
דאָ זיַינען מערן, זיסע פֿעפּערס, שאַלאַטן, און רעטעכער אין מיַין סאַלאַט.

It's not hard to grow tomatoes.
es iz nisht shver tsu vaksn pomidorn.
עס איז נישט שווער צו וואַקסן פּאָמידאָרן.

Eggplant can be cooked or fried.
patlezhan ken zeyn gekokht oder gepreglt.
פּאַטלעזשאַן קען זיַין געקאָכט אָדער געפּרעגלט.

I like beets in my salad.
ikh hob lib burikes s in meyn salat.
איך האָב ליב בורעקעס אין מיַין סאַלאַט.

I don't like to eat hot peppers.
ikh hob nisht lib tsu esn sharfe fefers.
איך האָב נישט ליב צו עסן שאַרפֿע פֿעפּערס.

Celery - tselerie צעלעריִע
Spinach - shpinat שפּינאַט
Cabbage - kroyt קרויט
Cauliflower - kolifior קאָליפֿיאָר
Beans – beblekh בעבלעך
Corn - papshoy פּאַפּשוי
Garlic - knobl קנאָבל
Onion - tsibele ציבעלע
Artichoke - artitshok אַרטיטשאָק
Grilled vegetables – grilirte grinsn גרילירטע גרינסן
Steamed vegetables – gedemfte grinsn געדעמפֿטע גרינסן

Celery and spinach have natural vitamins.
tselerie un shpinat hobn natirlekhe vitaminen.
צעלעריִע און שפּינאַט האָבן נאַטירלעכע וויטאַמינען

Fried cauliflower tastes better than fried cabbage.
gepreglte kalefior shmekt beser vi gepreglte kroyt.
געפּרעגלטע קאָליפֿיאָר שמעקט בעסער ווי געפּרעגלטע קרויט.

Rice and beans are my favorite side dish.
rayz aun beblekh zenen meyn balibste zayt maykhl.
רייַז און בעבלעך זענען מייַן באַליבסטע זייַט מאכל.

I like butter on corn.
ikh hob lib puter af papshoy.
איך האָב ליב פּוטער אויף פּאַפּשוי.

Garlic is an important ingredient in many cuisines.
knobl iz a vikhtike ingridyant in a sakh maykholim.
קנאָבל איז אַ וויכטיקע ינגרידיאַנט אין אַ סך מאכלים.

Where is the onion powder?
vu iz di tsibele proshik?
ווו איז די ציבעלע פּראָשיק?

An artichoke is difficult to peel.
a artitshok iz shver tsu sheyln.
אַ אַרטיטשאָק איז שווער צו שיילן.

Cucumber – ugerke אוגערקע
Lentils - lindzn לינדזן
Peas - arbes ארבעס
Green onion – grine tsibele גרינע ציבעלע
Herbs - kraytikhser קרייַטיכסער
Basil - bazilik באַזיליק
Parsley - petreshke פּעטרעשקע
Cilantro - feld-gliander פֿעלד־גליאַנדער
Dill - krop קראָפּ
Mint - mints מינץ
Potato – kartofl קאַרטאָפּל
Sweet Potato – batate באַטאַטע

I want to order lentil soup.
ikh vilbashteln lindzn zup.
.איך וויל באַשטעלן לינדזן זופ

Please put the green onion in the refrigerator.
bite leyg di grine tsibele in frijider.
ביטע לייג די גרינע ציבעלע אין פרידזשידער.

The most common kitchen herbs are basil, cilantro, dill, parsley, and mint.
di merst bakante kraytekhser zenen bazilik, feld-gliander, krop, petreshke un mints.
,די מערסטע באַקאַנטע קרייַטעכסער קיך זענען באַזיליק, פֿעלד־גליאַנדער, קראָפ
.פּעטרעשקע, און מינץ

Some of the most common vegetables for tempura are sweet potatoes and mushrooms.
etlekhe fun di merste proste grinsn far tempura zenen batates un shvemlekh.
עטלעכע פון די מערסטע פּראָסטע גרינסן פֿאַר טעמפּוראַ זענען באַטאַטעס און
.שוועמלעך

I want to order vegetarian sushi with asparagus and cucumber along with a side of seaweed salad.
ikh vil bashtelnvegetaryer sushi mit sparzhe aun ugerke tsuzamen mit a zayt fun yam - groz salat.
איך וויל באַשטעלן סושי מיט ספּאַרזשע און אוגערקע צוזאַמען מיט אַ זייַט פון ים -
.גראָז סאַלאַט

Mushroom – shveml שוועמל
Asparagus - sparzhe ספּאַרזשע
Seaweed – yam - groz גראָז - ים
Pumpkin – kirbes קירבעס
Squash - kabak קאַבאַק
Zucchini - tsukini צוקיני
Chickpeas – arbes ארבעס
Vegetable garden – gorten grinsen גאָרטן גרינסן

I enjoy eating pumpkin seeds as a snack.
Ikh hob lib tsu esn kirbes zamen vi a farbaysn.
איך האָב ליב צו עסן קירבעס זאמען ווי אַ פֿאַרבײַסן.

I must water my vegetable garden.
ikh muz bavasernmayn grinsn gortn.
איך מוז באַוואַסערן מײַן גרינסן גאָרטן

The potatoes in the field are ready to harvest.
di kartofl inemfeld zenen greyt tsu klaybn.
די קאַרטאָפֿל אינעם פעלד זענען גרייט צו קלײַבן.

Chickpeas are a popular ingredient in Middle Eastern food.
Nahit is a populere ingridyant in mitl mzrkh esnvarg.
ארבעס איז אַ פּאָפּולערע אינגרעדיענט אינמיטל מזרח עסנוואַרג

Is there zucchini in the soup?
iz do tsukini in di zup?
איז דאָ צוקיני אין די זופ?

I like to put ginger dressing on my salad.
ikh hob lib tsu leygn ingber sos aoyf meyn salat.
איך האָב ליב צו לייגן אינגבער סאס אויף מיין סאַלאַט.

The tomatoes are fresh but the cucumbers are rotten.
di tamatn zenen frish ober di ugerkes zenen paskudne.
די טאמאטן זענען פריש אבער די אוגערקעס זענען פּאסקודנע

FRUIT - FRUKHT רפוטכ

Apple - epl עפל
Orange - marants מאַראַנץ
Grapefruit - grefrukht גרעפּפֿרוכט
Peach - fershke פּערשקע
Tropical fruit - tropishe frukht טראָפּישעפּרוכט
Papaya - papeya פּאַפּייאַ
Coconut - kokosnus קאָקאָסנוס
Cherry - karsh קערש

Can I add raisins to the apple pie?
ken ikh tsugebn roszhinkes in dem epl pay?
קען איך צוגעבן ראָזשינקעס אין דעם עפל פּײַ?

Orange juice is a wonderful source of Vitamin C.
marants zaft iz a vunderlekh makor fun vitamin si.
מאַראַנץ זאַפֿט איז אַ ווונדערלעכע מקור פֿון וויטאַמין סי.

Grapefruits are extremely beneficial for your health.
grepfrukhtn zaynen zeyer gutfar dem gezunt.
גרעפּפֿרוכטן זײַנען זייער גוט פֿאַרן געזונט.

I have a peach tree in my front yard
ikh hob a fershke boym in meyn hoyf
איך האָב אַ פּערשקע בוים אין מיין הויף

I bought papayas and coconuts at the supermarket to prepare a fruit salad.
ikh hob gekoyft papeyas un kokosnus in supermark tsu makhn a frukht salat.
איך האָב געקויפֿט פּאַפּייאַס און קאָקאָסנוס אין סופּערמאַרק צו מאַכן אַ פּרוכט סאַלאַט.

I want to travel to Japan to see the famous cherry blossom.
ikh vil forn keyn yapan tsu zen di barimte karshnblumn.
איך וויל פֿאָרן קיין יאַפּאַן צו זען די באַרימטע קאַרשנבלומן.

Banana - banane באַנאַנע
Raisins - rozshinkes ראָזשינקעס
Prune - prune פרונע
Dates - teytl טייטל
Fig - fayg פֿײַג
Fruit salad - frukht salat פרוכט סאַלאַט
Dried fruit - getrikinte frukht געטריקענטע פרוכט
Apricot - aprikos אַפּריקאָס
Pear - barne באַרנע
Avocado - avokado אַוואָקאַדאָ
Ripe - tsaytig צײַטיג

A banana is a tropical fruit.
Banane zenen tropishe frukht.
אַ באַנאַנע איז אַ טראָפּישע פרוכט.

I want to mix dates and figs in my fruit salad.
ikh vil mishn teytln un faygn in meyn frukht salat.
איך וויל מישן טייטלן און פֿײַגן אין מיין פרוכט סאַלאַט.

Apricots and prunes are my favorite dried fruits.
aprikosn un prunz zenen meyn balibste fartriknte frukhtn.
אַפּריקאָטן און פרונז זענען מיין באַליבסטע פֿאַרטריקנטע פרוכטן.

Pears are delicious.
barnes zenen geshmak.
באַרנעס זענען געשמאַק.

The avocado isn't ripe yet.
di avokado iz nokh nisht tsaytik.
די אַוואָקאַדאָ איז נאָך נישט צײַטיק.

The green apple is very sour.
di grine epl iz zeyer zoyer.
די גרינע עפל איז זייער זויער.

The unripe peach is usually bitter.
nisht tsaytike sfershke zaynen geveyntlekh biter.
נישט צײַטיקע פֿערשקעס זײַנען געוויינטלעך ביטער

Fruit tree - frukht boym פרוכט בוים
Citrus - sitrus סיטרוס
Lemon - limene לימענע
Lime - laym ליים
Pineapple - ananas אַנאַנאַס
Melon - melon מעלאָן
Watermelon - kavene קאַוװענע
Plum - floym פלוים

How much does the watermelon juice cost?
vi fil kost di kavene zaft?
?ווי פיל קאָסט די קאַוװענע זאַפט

I have a pineapple plant in a pot.
ikh hob an ananas geviks in a top.
.איך האָב אַן אַנאַנאַס געוויקס אין אַ טאָפ

Melons grow on the ground.
melonen vaksn af der erd.
.מעלאָנען וואַקסן אויף דער ערד

I am going to the fruit-tree section of the nursery today to purchase a few citrus trees.
haynt gey ikh koyfn a por sitrus beymer
היַינט גיי איך קויפֿן אַ פּאָר סיטרוס בײַמער

I add either lemon juice or lime juice to my salad.
ikh leyg limene zaft oder laym zaft in meyn salat.
.איך לייג לימענע זאַפט אָדער ליַים זאַפט אין מיַין סאַלאַט

Plums are seasonal fruits.
floymn zaynen sizanal frukhtn.
.פלוימן זיַינען סיזאַנאַל פרוכטן

Strawberry - truskavke טרוסקאַװקע
Berry – yagde יאַגדע
Blueberry - yagdes יאַגדעס
Raspberry - malene מאַלענע
Grapes - troybn טרויבן
Pomegranate - milgroym מילגרוים
Olive - masline מאַסלינע
Grove – sod סאָד

Strawberries grow during the spring.
truskafkes vaksn in friling.
טרוסטטאַפֿקעס װאַקסן אין פֿרילינג.

Blueberry juice is very sweet.
yagde zaft iz zeyer zis.
יאַגדע.זאַפֿט איז זייער זיס

There are many raspberries growing on the bush.
a sakh malenes vaksn afn kust
אַ סך מאַלענעס װאַקסן אױפֿן קוסט

I need to pick the grapes to make the wine.
ikh darf klaybn di vayntroybn tsu makhn di vayn.
איך דאַרף קלײַבן די װײַנטרױבן צו מאַכן די װײַן.

Pomegranate juice contains a very high level of antioxidants.
milgroym zaft hot zeyer a sakh antyaxadants.
מילגרוים זאַפֿט האָט זייער אַ סך אַנטיאָקסעדענטן.

I have an olive grove in my backyard.
ikh hob a masline sod in meyn hoyf.
איך האָב אַ מאַסלינע סאָד אין מײן הױף.

SHOPPING - AYNKOYFN אײַנקױפֿן

Clothes - kleyder קלײדער
Clothing store - kleyder-gesheft קלײדער־געשעפט
For sale - tsum koyfn צום קױפֿן
Hat - hitl היטל
Shirt - hemd העמד
Shoes - shikh שיך
Skirt - kleydl קלײדל
Dress - kleyd קלײד
Pants - hoyzn הױזן
Shorts - kurtse hoyzn קורצע הױזן
Uniform - mundir מונדיר

There are a lot of clothes for sale today.
s'iz do a sakh kleyder af a hanukhe haynt
ס׳איז דאָ אַ סך קלײדער אױף אַ הנחה הײַנט

Does this hat look good?
zet dem hitl oys gut
זעט דעם היטל אױס גוט

I am happy with this shirt and these shoes.
ikh bin tsufridn mit dem hemd aun di shikh.
איך בין צופֿרידן מיט דעם העמד און די שיך.

She prefers a skirt instead of a dress.
zi vil beser a kleydl vi a kleyd.
זי װיל בעסער אַ קלײדל װי אַ קלײד

These pants aren't my size.
di hoyzn zenen nisht meyn greys.
די הױזן זענען נישט מײן גרײס.

There are uniforms for school at the clothing store.
es iz do shule mondirn in kleyder krom.
עס איז דאָ שולע מאַנדירן אין דער קלײדער קראָם

Suit - antsug אנצוג
Vest - vestl וועסטל
Tie - kravat קראוואַט
Belt - gartl גאַרטל
Socks - zokn זאָקן
Gloves - hentshkes הענטשקעס
Glasses - briln ברילן
Sunglasses - zunbriln זונברילן
Size - greys גרייס
Small - kleyn קליין
Medium - mitl מיטל
Large - groys גרויס
Thick - dik דיק
Thin - din דין
Thrift store - tendleray טענדלערײַ

I forgot my socks, belt, and shorts at your house.
ikh hob fargesn meyne zokn, mayn gartl un mayne kurtse hoyzn in deyn hoyz.
איך האב פארגעסן מיינע זאָקן, מײַן גאַרטל און מײַנע קורצע הויזן אין דיין הויז.

These gloves are a size too small. Do you have a medium size?
di o hentshkes zenen a greys tsu kleyn. Hot ir a mitl greys?
די הענטשעקס זענען אַ גרייס צו קליין. האָט איר אַ מיטל גרייס?

Today I don't need my reading glasses. However, I have my sunglasses.
haynt darf ikh nisht mayne leyn briln, ober ikh hob yo mayne zunbriln.
הײַנט דאַרף איך נישט מײַנע ליין ברילן, אָבער איך האָב יאָ מײַנע זונברילן

Where can I find a thrift store? I want to buy a suit, a vest, and a tie.
vu ken ikh gefinen a tendleray? ikh vil koyfn an antsug, a vestl aun a kravat.
ווו קען איך געפֿינען אַ טענדלערײַ? איך וויל קויפֿן אַן אַנצוג, אַ וועסטל, און אַ קראַוואַט

Jacket - rekl רעקל

Scarf - shal שאַל

Mittens - kulikleh קוליקלעך

Sleeve - arbl אַרבל

Boots (rain, winter) - shtivl שטיוול

Sweater - sveter סוועטער

Bathing suit – bod kostum באַד קאָסטום

Flip flops - fingershikh פֿינגערשיך

Tank top – hemd on arbl העמד אָן אַרבל

Sandals - sandaln סאַנדאַלן

Heels – hoykhe knafl הויכע קנאַפֿל

We are going to the mountain today so don't forget your jacket, mittens, and scarf.

mir geyn tsu dem barg haynt iz farges nisht deyn rekl, kuliklekh un shal.

.מיר גיין צום באַרג היַינט איז פֿאַרגעס נישט דיין רעקל, קוליקלעך און שאַל

I have long sleeve shirts and short sleeve shirts.

ikh hob lange arbl hemder aun kurtse arbl hemder.

.איך האָב לאַנגע אַרבל העמדער און קורצע אַרבל העמדער

Boots and sweaters are meant for winter.

shtivl un sveterz zenen gemeynt far vinter.

.שטיוול און סוועטערז זענען געמיינט פֿאַר ווינטער

At the beach, I wear a bathing suit and flip flops.

Baym plazshe trog ikh a bod kostum un fingershikh.

.ביַים פּלאַזשע,טראָג איך אַ באַד קאָסטום און פֿינגערשיך

I want to buy a tank top for summer.

ikh vil koyfn a hemd on arbl far zumer.

.איך וויל קויפֿן אַ העמד אָן אַרבל פֿאַר זומער

I can't wear heels on the beach, only sandals.

ikh ken nisht trognhoykhe knafl afn plazshe, nor sandaln.

.איך קען נישט טראָגן הויכע קנאַפֿל אויפֿן פּלאַזשע, נאָר סאַנדאַלן

On sale - af an onbot אויף אן אָנבאָט
Expensive - tayer טייער
Free - umzist אומזיסט
Discount - hanokhe הנחה
Cheap - bilik ביליק
Shopping - aynkoyfn איינקויפֿן
Mall – aynkoyf tsenter איינקויף צענטער

What will be on sale tomorrow?
vos vet zeyn aoyf an onbotmorgn?
וואָס וועט זיין אויף אן אָנבאָט מאָרגן?

This is free.
dos iz umzist.
דאָס איז אומזיסט.

Even though this cologne and this perfume are discounted, they are still very expensive.
khotsh di keln aun dem parfum zenen af an onbot zaynen zey nokh alts zeyer tayer.
כאָטש די קעלן און דעם פֿאַרפֿום זענען אן אָנבאָט אויף זיי זיינען נאָך אַלץ זייער טייער.

These items are very cheap.
di zakhn zenen zeyer bilik.
די זאכן זענען זייער ביליק.

I can go shopping only on weekends.
ikh ken geyn aynkoyfn bloyz beshas sofvokh.
איך קען גיין איינקויפֿן בלויז בשעת סוף וואך.

Is the local mall far?
iz di hige aynkoyf tsenter vayt?
איז די לאָקאַלע איינקויף צענטער ווייט?

Store - krom קראָם

Business hours - gesheft sheh געשעפט שעה

Open - ofn אָפֿן

Closed - farmakht פֿארמאכט

Entrance - arayngang אַרײַנגאַנג

Exit - aroysgang אַרויסגאַנג

Shopping cart - aynkoyf vegele אײַנקויף וועגעלע

Shopping basket - aynkoyf koysh אײַנקויף קויש

Shopping bag – aynkoyf baytl אײַנקויף בײַטל

Toy store - shpilikhl krom שפּיליכל קראָם

Toy - shpilikhl שפּיליכל

Book store - bikher krom ביכער קראָם

What are your (plural) **business hours?**

vos zenen ayere gesheft sheh?

וואָס זענען אײַערע געשעפט שעה?

What time does the store open?

vifl azeyger efnt der krom

וויפֿל אַזייגער עפֿנט דער קראָם

What times does the store close?

vifl azeyger farmakht der krom

וויפֿל אַזייגער פֿאַרמאַכט דער קראָם

Where is the entrance?

vu iz der arayngang?

ווו איז דער אַרײַנגאַנג?

Where is the exit?

vu iz der aroysgang?

ווו איז דער אַרויסגאַנג?

My children want to go to the toy store so they can fill up the shopping cart with toys.

meyne kinder viln geyn in shpilikhlkrom khdi zey zaln kenen anfiln dem eynkoyfn vegele mit shpilikhlekh.

מיינע קינדער ווילן גיין אין שפּיליכל קראָם כדי זיי זאלן קענען אנפילן דעם אײַנקויפֿן וועגעלע מיט שפּיליכלעך.

Music store - muzik krom מוזיק קראָם
Jeweler - yuvelir יוּוועליר
Jewelry - tsirung צירונג
Gold - Gold גאָלד
Silver - zilber זילבער
Necklace - keytl קייטל
Bracelet - braslet בראַסלעט
Diamond - diament דיאַמענט
Gift – matone מתּנה
Coin - matbeye מטבע
Antique - antik אַנטיק
Dealer - hendler העָנדלער

I use a large shopping basket at the supermarket.
ikh nits a groyse aynkoyf koysh in di supermark.
.איך ניץ אַ גרויסע אײַנקויף קויש אין די סופּערמאַרק

There is a sale at the bookstore right now.
es iz an onbot in di buxtor itst.
.עס איז אַן אָנבאָט אין ביכער קראָם איצט

The jeweler sells gold and silver.
der ivuelir farkoyft gold un zilber.
.דער יוּוועליר פֿאַרקויפֿט גאָלד און זילבער

I want to buy a diamond necklace.
ikh vil koyfn a diment keytl.
.איך וויל קויפֿן אַ דיאַמענט קייטל

This bracelet and those pair of earrings are gifts for my daughter.
dem braslet aun di por oyringlekh zenen matones far meyn tokhter.
.דעם בראַסלעט און די פּאָר אײַרינגלעך זענען מתּנות פֿאַר מיין טאָכטער

He is an antique coin dealer.
er iz an antik matbeye hendler.
ער איז אַן אַנטיק מטבע העָנדלער

FAMILY - MISHPOKHE משפחה

Mother - mame מאמע
Father - tate טאַטע
Son - zun זון
Daughter - tokhter טאכטער
Brother - Bruder ברודער
Sister - shvester שוועסטער
Husband - man מאַן
Wife - froy פרוי
Parents (plural) - Eltern עלטערן
Child - kind קינד
Baby - eyfele עופֿעלע

I have a big family.
ikh hob a groyse mshfkhh.
איך האב א גרויסע משפחה.

My brother and sister are here.
mayn bruder un mayn shvester zenen do.
מיין ברודער און מיַין שוועסטער זענען דא.

The mother and father want to spend time with their child.
di mame un tateviln farbrengen tseyt mit zeyer kind.
די מאַמע און טאַטע ווילן פֿאַרברענגען צייט מיט זייער קינד.

He wants to bring his son and daughter to the public park.
er vil brengen zeyn zun un zayn tokhter in park.
ער וויל ברענגען זיין זון און זיַין טאַכטער אין פּאַרק.

The husband and wife have a new baby.
der man un froy hobn a naye eyfele.
דער מאַן און פרוי האָבן אַ נייַע עופֿעלע.

Grandfather - zeyde זיידע
Grandmother - bobe באָבע
Grandparents - zeyde-bobe זיידע-באָבע
Grandson - eynikl אייניקל
Granddaughter - eynikl אייניקל
Grandchildren - eyniklekh אייניקלעך
Nephew – plimenik פּלימעניק
Niece – plimenitse פּלימעניצע
Cousin - shvesterkind שוועסטערקינד

The grandfather wants to take his grandson to the movie.
der zeyde vil nemen zayn eynikl tsum film.
דער זיידע וויל נעמען זײַן אייניקל צום פֿילם.

The grandmother wants to give her granddaughter money.
di bobe vil gebn ir eynikl gelt.
די באָבע וויל געבן איר אייניקל געלט.

The grandparents want to spend time with their grandchildren.
di zeyde-bobe viln farbrengen tseyt mit zeyere eyniklekh.
די זיידע-באָבע ווילן פֿאַרברענגען צייט מיט זייערע אייניקלעך.

I want to go to the park with my niece and nephew.
ikh vil geyn in park mit meyn plimenitse un plimenik.
איך וויל גיין אין פּאַרק מיט מיין פּלימעניצע און פּלימעניק.

My cousin wants to see his children.
meyn shvesterkind vil zen zeyne kinder.
מיין שוועסטערקינד וויל זען זיינע קינדער.

That man is a good parent.
der mentsh iz a guter tate.
דער מענטש איז אַ גוטער טאַטע.

Aunt - mume מומע

Uncle - feter פעטער

Man - man מאַן

Woman - froy פרוי

Stepfather - shtiftate שטיפֿטאַטע

Stepmother - shtifmame שטיפֿמאַמע

Stepbrother - shtifbruder שטיפֿברודער

Stepsister - shtifshevester שטיפֿשוועסטער

Stepson - shtifzun שטיפֿזון

Stepdaughter - shtiftokhter שטיפֿטאָכטער

In laws - mkhutnim מחותּנים

Ancestors - oves אָבֿות

Family tree - mshpkhh boym משפּחה בוים

Generation - dur דור

First born - ersht geboyrn ערשט געבוירן

Only child - eyntsik kind איינציק קינד

My aunt and uncle came here for a visit.
meyn mume un feter zenen gekumen aher mir tsu bazukhn.
מײַן מומע און פעטער זענען געקומען אהער מיר צו באַזוכן.

He is their only child.
er iz zeyer eyntsike kind.
ער איז זייער איינציקע קינד.

My wife is pregnant with twins.
mayn froy shvangert mit tsviling.
מײַן פרוי שוואַנגערט מיט צווילינג.

He is their eldest son.
er iz zeyer eltster zun.
ער איז זייער עלטסטער זון.

The first-born child usually takes on all the responsibilities.
der ershter-geboyrn kind nemt geveyntlekh on ale di akhrayesin.
דער ערשטער-געבוירן קינד נעמט געווײַנטלעך אָן אַלע די אַחריותים.

Relative - korev קרוב
Family member - mishpokhe glid משפחה גליד
Twins - tsviling צווילינג
Pregnant - trogedik טראָגעדיק
Adopted child - adoptirte kind אַדאָפּטירטע קינד
Orphan - isum יתום
Adult - dervaksn דערוואַקסן
Neighbor - shokhn שכן
Friend - khaver חבר
Roommate - mitvoyner מיטוווינער

I was able to find all my relatives and ancestors on my family tree.
ikh hob gekent gefinen ale mayne kruvim aun ovus aoyf mayn
mshpkhh-boym.
איך האָב געקענט געפֿינען אַלע מײַנע קרובֿים און אָבֿות אויף מײַן משפּחה־בוים.

My parents' generation loved disco music.
mayne eltern dur hot lib gehat diskomuzik.
מײַנע עלטערנס דור האָט ליב געהאַט דיסקאָמוזיק.

Their adopted child was an orphan
zeyer adoptirte kind iz geven a yosm
זייער אַדאָפּטירטע קינד איז געווען אַ יתום

I like my in-laws.
ikh hob lib mayne mkhutnim.
איך האָב ליב מײַנע מחותּנים.

I have a nice neighbor.
ikh hob a sheyne shokhn.
איך האָב אַ שיינע שכן.

She considers her stepson as her real son.
zi batrakht ir shtif zun vi ir emesn zun.
זי באַטראַכט איר שטיפֿ זון ווי איר אמתן זון.

She is his stepdaughter.
zi iz zeyn shtif-takhter.
זי איז זיין שטיפֿ־טאָכטער.

HUMAN BODY - KERPER קערפער

Head - kop קאָפּ
Face - pnim פּנים
Eye - oyg אויג /(p) oygn אויגן
Ear - oyer אויער /(p) oyern אויערן
Nose - noz נאָז
Mouth - moyl מויל
Lips - lipn ליפּן

My chin, cheeks, mouth, lips, and eyes are all part of my face.
mayn gombe, bakn, moyl, lipn un oygn zenen ale teyl fun meyn ponim.
מײַן גאָמבע ,באַקן ,מויל, ליפּן און אויגן זענען אלע אַ טייל פון מיין פנים.

He has small ears.
er hot kleyne aoyern.
ער האָט קלײַנע אויערן.

I have a cold so therefore my nose, eyes, mouth, and tongue are affected.
ikh hobn a farkilung iz meyn noz, oygn, moyl, aun tsung zenen afektad.
איך האָב אַ פֿאַרקילונג איז מיין נאָז ,אויגן, מויל ,און צונג זענען אַפעקטאַד.

The five senses are sight, touch, taste, smell, and hearing.
di finf khushn zenen zen, onrirn, shmekn, shmekn aun hern.
די פֿינף חושן זענען זען, אָנרירן, שמעקן, געשמאַק, און הערן.

I am washing my face right now.
ikh vash meyn pnim yetst.
איך וואַש מיין פנים יעצט.

I have a headache
ikh hob a kopveytuk
איך האָב אַ קאָפּווייטוק

My eyebrows are too long.
meyne bremen zenen tsu lang.
מײַנע ברעמען זענען צו לאַנג.

Tongue - tsung צונג
Cheek - bak באַק
Chin - gombe גאָמבע
Neck - nakn נאַקן
Throat - haldz האַלדז
Forehead - shtern שטערן
Eyebrow - brem ברעם
Eyelashes - vyes וויעס
Hair - hor האָר
Beard - bord באָרד
Mustache - vontses וואָנצעס
Tooth - tson צאָן / (p) tseyn ציין
Skin - hoyt הויט

He must shave his beard and mustache.
er muz opgoln di bord aun di vontses.
.ער מוז אָפּגאָלן די באָרד און די וואָנצעס

I brush my teeth every morning.
ikh barsht meyne tseyn yeder fri.
.איך באַרשט מיינע ציין יעדער פֿרי

She puts makeup on her cheeks and a lot of lipstick on her lips.
zi leygt shminke oyf di bakn un a sakh lipn pomade oyf di lipn.
.זי לייגט שמינקע אויף די באַקן און אַ סך ליפּן פּאָמאַדע אויף די ליפּן

Her hair covered her forehead.
di hor hot badekt ir shtern.
.די האָר האָט באַדעקט איר שטערן

She has a long neck.
zi hat a langn nakn.
.זי האַט אַ לאַנגן נאַקן

I have a sore throat.
Mayn haldz tut vey.
מײַן האַלדז טוט ווײי

I have beautiful skin.
ikh hob sheyne hoyt.
.איך האָב שיינע הויט

Shoulder - axl אַקסל

Chest - brust ברוסט

Arm - orem אָרעם

Hand - hant האַנט

Palm (of hand) - dlonye דלאָניע

Elbow - elnboygn עלנבויגן

Wrist - hantgelenk האַנטגעלענק

Finger - Finger פינגער

Thumb - grober finger גראָבער פינגער

Back - rukn רוקן

Belly - boykh בויך

Stomach - mogn מאָגן

Intestines - gederem געדערעם

Brain - mukh מוח

Heart - harts האַרץ

Kidneys – niren נירן

Lungs - lungen לונגען

Liver - leber לעבער

He has a problem with his stomach.
er hat a problem mit zeyn mogn.
ער האָט אַ פּראָבלעם מיט זיין מאָגן.

The brain, heart, kidneys, lungs, and liver are internal organs.
der moyekh, harts, niren, lungen un leber zenen organen.
דער מוח, האַרץ, נירן, לונגען און לעבער זענען אָרגאַנען.

His chest and shoulders are very muscular.
zeyn brust aun pleytses zenen zeyer maskyaler.
זיין ברוסט און פּלייצעס זענען זייער מאַסקיאַלער.

I need to strengthen my arms and legs.
ikh darf farshtarkn di hent aun di fis.
איך דאַרף פאַרשטאַרקן די הענט און די פיס.

I accidentally hit his wrist with my elbow.
ikh hob al-pi toes geplapt zeyn hantgelenk mit meyn elnboygn.
איך האָב על־פי טעות געקלאַפּט זיין האַנטגעלענק מיט מיין עלנבויגן.

Leg - fus פוס
Ankle - knekhl קנעכל
Foot - fis פֿיס
Palm (of foot) - dlonye דלאָניע
Toe - fusfinger פוספֿינגער
Nail - nogl נאָגל
Joint - gelenk געלענק
Muscle - muskl מוסקל
Skeleton - skelet סקעלעט
Spine - ruknbeyn רוקנביין / **Ribs** - ribs ריבן
Bone - beyn ביין
Skull - sharbn שאַרבן
Vein - oder אָדער

I have pain in every part of my body especially in my hand, ankle, and back.
ikh hob aveytik in yeder teyl fun meyn guf spetsyel in meyn hant, knekhl aun rukn.
איך האָב אַ ווייטיק אין יעדער טייל פון מיין גוף ספּעציעל אין מיין האַנט, קנעכל און רוקן.

I want to cut my nails.
ikh vil shneydn di negl.
איך וויל שניידן די נעגל.

I need a new bandage for my thumb.
ikh darf a nay bandazh far meyn grober finger.
איך דאַרף אַ ניי באַנדאַזש פֿאַר מיין גראָבער פֿינגער.

I have a cast on my foot because of a broken bone.
kh'hab a gips aoyfn fus tsulib a tsebrakhn beyn.
כ'האב אַ גיפּס אויפֿן פֿוס צוליב אַ צעבראָכן ביין.

I have muscles and joint pain today.
haynt tun mayne musklin un mayne gelenkn vey
היַינט טון מיַינע מוסקלען און מיַינע געלענקן וויי

The spine is the main part of the body.
di ruknbeyn iz der hoypt teyl fun dem guf.
די רוקנביין איז דער הויפּט טייל פון דעם גוף.

HEALTH AND MEDICAL
GEZUNT UN MEDITSINISH געזונט און מעדיציניש

Disease - krenk קרענק
Bacteria - baktirya באַקטיריאַ
Sick - Krank קראָנק
Clinic - klinik קליניק
Headache - kopveytik קאָפּווייטיק
Earache - aoyerveytik אויערווייטיק
Pharmacy - apteyk אַפּטייק
Prescription - retsept רעצעפּט
Symptoms - simptomim סימפּטאָמים
Nausea - ekl עקל
Stomachache – boykh veytig בויך ווייטיג
Allergy - alergye אַלערגיע

Are you in good health?
bistu gezunt?
ביסטו געזונט?

These bacteria caused this disease.
di baktirya iz dem sibe far dem krenk.
די באַקטיריא איז דער סיבה פֿאַר דעם קרענק.

He is very sick.
er iz zeyer krank.
ער איז זייער קראָנק.

I have a headache so I must go to the pharmacy to refill my prescription.
ikh hob a kopveytik iz ikh muz geyn tsu di apteyk tsu rifiln meyn retsept.
איך האָב אַ קאָפּווייטיק איז איך מוז גיין צו די אַפּטייק צו ריפֿילן מיין רעצעפּט.

The main symptoms of food poisoning are nausea and stomachache.
di hoypt simptomim fun mogn farsamung zenen ekl aun mogn veytik.
די הויפּט סימפּטאָמים פֿון מאָגן־פֿאַרסאַמונג זענען עקל און מאָגן ווייטיק.

Penicillin - penisilin פעניסילין
Antibiotic - antibyotik אַנטיביאָטיק
Sore throat - haldzveytik האַלדזווייטיק
Fever - hits היץ
Flu - flu פלו
Cough - hust הוסט
To cough - tsu hust צו הוסט
Infection - infektsye אינפעקציע
Injury - shodn שאָדן
Scar - shram שראַם
Ache / pain - veytik ווייטיק
Intensive care - intensive ophit אינטענסיווע אָפהיט
Band-Aid / **bandage** - bandazh באַנדאַזש

I have an allergy to penicillin, so I need another antibiotic.
ikh hob a alergye tsu penisillin, iz darf ikh an ander antibyotik.
איך האָב אַן אַלערגיע צו פעניסילין, איז דאַרף איך אן אנדער אַנטיביאָטיק.

What do I need to treat an earache?
vos darf ikh tsu bahandlen an oyerveytik?
וואָס דאַרף איך צו באַהאַנדלען אַן אויערווייטיק?

I need to go to the clinic for my fever and sore throat.
ikh darf geyn in klinik far meyn hits un haldzveytig.
איך דאַרף גיין אין קליניק פֿאַר מיין היץ און האַלדזווייטיג.

The bandage won't help your infection.
di bandazh vet nisht helfn deyn infektsye.
די באַנדאַזש וועט נישט העלפֿן דיין אינפעקציע.

I have a serious injury so I must go to intensive care.
ikh hob a ernste shodn iz ikh muz geyn in intensive zorgn.
איך האָב אַן ערנסטע שאָדן איז איך מוז גיין אין אינטענסיווע זאָרגן.

I have muscle and joint pains today.
ikh hob muskl aun gelenk veytikn haynt.
איך האָב מוסקל און געלענק ווייטיקן היינט.

Hospital - shpital שפּיטאל
Doctor - dokter דאָקטער
Nurse - kranknshvester קראַנקנשוועסטער
Family Doctor - mshpkhh dokter משפּחה דאָקטער
Pediatrician - pidyatrishan פּידיאַטרישאַן
Medication - meditsin מעדיצין
Pills - piln פּילן
Heartburn - brenenish ברענעניש
Paramedic - paramedic פּאַראַמעדיק
Emergency room - neytfal tsimer נייטפֿאַל צימער
Health insurance - gezunt farzikherung געזונט פֿאַרזיכערונג
Patient - patsient פּאַציענט
Surgery - khirugie כירוגיע
Surgeon - khirurg כירורג
Face mask - pnim maske פּנים מאַסקע
Anesthesia - anistizha אַניסטיזשא
Local anesthesia - lakale anistizha לאָקאַלע אַניסטיזשא
General anesthesia - algemeyne anistizha אַלגעמיינע אַניסטיזשא

Where is the closest hospital?
vu iz der nentster shpital?
?וווּ איז דער נענטסטער שפּיטאל

Usually we see the nurse before the doctor.
gevenlikh zeen mir di krankenshvester farn dokter.
געוועגליך זעען מיר די קראַנקענשוועסטער פֿאַרן דאָקטער.

The paramedics can take her to the emergency room but she doesn't have health insurance.
di paramediks kenen ir nemen in noytfal tsimer ober zi tut nisht hobn gezunt farzikherung.
די פּאַראַמעדיקס קענען איר נעמען אין נייטפֿאַל צימער אָבער זי טוט נישט האָבן געזונט פֿאַרזיכערונג.

The doctor treated the patient.
der dokter hat bahandlt dem patsyent.
דער דאָקטער האָט באַהאַנדלט דעם פּאַציענט.

He needs knee surgery today.
er darf heynt a kni-operatsye.
ער דאַרף היינט אַ קני-אָפּעראַציע.

114

Wheelchair - rederbenkl רעדערבענקל'
Cane - shtekn שטעקן
Walker - voker וואָקער
Stretcher - strettsher סטרעטטשער
Dialysis - dyalisis דיאַליסיס / **Insulin -** Insulin ינסולין
Diabetes - tsukerkrenk צוקערקרענק
Temperature - temperatur טעמפּעראַטור
Thermometer - termometer טערמאָמעטער
A shot – aynshpritsung אײַנשפּריצונג
Needle - nodl נאָדל / **Syringe -** shprits שפּריץ
In need of - in noyt fun אין נויט פון

The surgeon needs to administer general anesthesia in order to operate on the patient.
der khirurg darf gebn general anistizha tsu kenen operirn oyf di patsyent.
דער כירורג דאַרף געבן גענעראַל אַניסטיזשאַ צו קענען אָפּערירן אויף די פּאַציענט.

Does the patient need a wheelchair or a stretcher?
darf der patsyent a rederbenkl oder a trogbetl?
דאַרף דער פּאַציענט אַ רעדערבענקל אָדער אַ טראָגבעטל?

I have to take medicine every day.
ikh muz nemen meditsin yeder tog.
איך מוז נעמען מעדיצין יעדער טאָג.

Do you have any pills for heartburn?
Tsi hot irpilz far brenenish?
צי האָט איר פּילז פאַר ברענעניש?

Where is the closest dialysis center?
vu iz di nenste dyalisis tsenter?
וווּ איז די נענסטע דיאַליסיס צענטער?

The doctor didn't prescribe insulin for my diabetes.
der dokter hot mir nisht gegebn insalan far meyn tsukerkrenk.
דער דאָקטער האָט מיר נישט געגעבן אינסולין פאַר מיין צוקערקרענק.

I need a thermometer to take my temperature.
ikh darf a termometer tsu nemen meyn temperatur.
איך דאַרף אַ טערמאָמעטער צו נעמען מיין טעמפּעראַטור.

Stroke - shlak שלאַק
Blood - blut בלוט
Blood pressure - blut druk בלוט דרוק
Heart attack - harts atake האַרץ אטאַקע
Cancer - rak ראַק
Chemotherapy - kimouterapi קימאָוטעראַפּי
Help - hilf הילף
Germs - germez גערמעז
Virus - Virus ווירוס
Vaccine - vaksine וואַקסינע
A cure - a refuah א רפואה / **To cure** - tsu heyln צו היילן
Cholesterol - kalesteral קאַלעסטעראַל
Nutrition - dernerung דערנערונג
Diet - diete דיעטע
Blind - blind בלינד
Deaf - toyb טויב
Mute - shtum שטום

A stroke is caused by a lack of blood flow to the brain.
a shlak geshset tsulib a mangl fun blut loyfn tsu di moykh.
א שלאַק געשעט צוליב אַ מאַנגל פון בלוט לויפן צו די מוח.

These are the symptoms of a heart attack.
dos zenen di simptoms fun a harts atak.
דאָס זענען די סימפּטאָמס פון אַ האַרץ אטאַק.

Chemotherapy is for treating cancer.
kimouterapi iz far bahandlung a rak.
קימאָוטעראַפּי איז פאַר באַהאַנדלונג אַ ראַק.

Proper nutrition is very important, and you must avoid foods that are high in cholesterol.
gute dernerung iz zeyer vikhtik aun me muz oysmeydn esn vos iz hoykh in kalesteral.
גוטע דערנערונג איז זייער וויכטיק און מען מוז אויסמײַדן עסן וואָס איז הויך אין קאַלעסטעראַל.

I am starting my diet today.
ikh heyb on meyn dyete haynt.
איך הייב אָן מיין דיעטע הײַנט.

Young - yung יונג

Elderly - alt אַלט

Fat - fet פעט

Skinny (person) - dar דאַר

Nursing home – moyshev-zikeynim מושבֿ־זקנים

Disability - disabiliti דיסאַביליטי

Handicap – meniah מניעה

Paralysis - paralisis פּאַראַליסיס

Depression - depresye דעפּרעסיע / **Anxiety** - dayges דייַגעס

Dentist - tseyndokter ציינדאָקטער

X-rays - rentgen רענטגען

Tooth cavity – lekher in di tseyn לעכער אין די ציין

Toothpaste - tseyn paste ציין פּאַסטע

Toothbrush – tseyn bershtl ציין בערשטל

There is no cure for this virus, only a vaccine.
es iz nisht do keyn refue far dem virus, nor a vaktsin.
עס איז נישט דאָ קיין רפֿואה פֿאַר דעם ווירוס, נאָר אַ וואַקצין.

The nursing home is open 365 days a year.
di moyshev zkeynim iz ofn 365 teg a yor.
די מושבֿ־זקנים איז אָפֿן 365 טעג אַ יאָר.

I don't like suffering from depression and anxiety.
ikh hob nisht lib leydn fun depresye aun dayges.
איך האָב נישט ליב ליידן פֿון דעפּרעסיע און דאגות.

Soap and water kill germs.
zeyf aun vaser teytn germes.
זייף און וואַסער טייטן גערמעס.

The dentist took X-rays of my teeth to check for cavities.
der tseyndokter hot genumen rentgen fun meyn tseyn tsu kontrolirn far lekher.
דער ציינדאָקטער האָט גענומען רענטגען פֿון מײַנע ציין צו קאָנטראָלירן פֿאַר לעכער

In the morning I put toothpaste on my toothrbush.
in der fri ikh shteln tson pap aoyf meyn tseynbershtl.
אין דער פֿרי לייג איך ציין פּאַסטע אויף מײַן ציינבערשטל.

EMERGENCY & DISASTERS
NOYTFAL UN KATASTROFYE קאטאסטראפיע

Help – hilf הילף
Fire – fayer פייער
Ambulance – ambulans אמבולאנס
First aid - ershter hilf ערשטער הילף
CPR – CPR ספּר
Emergency number - noytfal numer נויטפאל נומער
Accident – sibe סיבה
Car crash – oyto sibe אויטא סיבה
Death – toyt טויט
Deadly – geferlekh געפֿערלעך
Fatality – toitfal טויטפאל
Lightly wounded – a bisl vey geton א ביסל וויי געטאן
Moderately wounded – vey geton וויי געטאן
Seriously wounded – shtark vey geton שטארק וויי געטאן

There is a fire. I need to call for help.
es iz do a fayer. ikh darf rufn hilf.
עס איז דא א פייער. איך דארף רופֿן הילף

I need to call an ambulance.
ikh darf rufn an ambulans.
איך דארף רופֿן אן אמבולאנס

That accident was bad.
der sibe iz geven shlekht.
דער סיבה איז געווען שלעכט

The car crash was fatal, there were two deaths, and four suffered serious injuries.
der oyto krakh iz geven fatal, es zenen geven tsvey toyte, aun fir hobn gelitn ernste vundn.
דער אויטא קראך איז געווען פאטאל, עס זענען געווען צוויי טויטע און פיר האבן געליטן ערנסטע ווונדן

One was moderately wounded and two were lightly wounded.
eyner iz geven farvaundet un tsvey zeynen leykht farvaundet gevarn.
איינער איז געווען פארווונדעט און צוויי זענען לייכט פארווונדעט געווארן

Firetruck – lesh oyto לעש אויטא
Siren – sirene סירענע
Fire extinguisher – feyerlesher פייער לעשער
Police – politsey פּאליציי
Police station - politsey stantsye פּאליציי סטאנסיע
Robbery – gneiva גנבה
Thief – ganev גנב
Murderer – merder מערדער

CPR is a first step of first-aid.
CPR iz der ershter trit fun ershter hilf.
ספר איז דער ערשטער טריט פון ערשטער הילף

Please provide me with the emergency number.
bite geb mir di noytfal numer.
ביטע, געב מיר די נויטפל נומער

The thief wants to steal my money.
der ganev vil ganvenen mayn gelt.
דער גנב וויל גנבנען מיין געלט

I must call the police station to report a robbery.
ikh muz rufn di politsey stantsye tsu meldn a gnibh.
איך מוז ריפן די פליציי סטאנסיע צו מעלדן א גנבה

The police are on their way.
di politsey zenen oyfn veg.
די פּאליציי זענען אויפן וועג

The siren of the fire truck is very loud.
di sirene funem leshoyto iz zeyer hoykh.
די סירענע פונם לעשויטאָ יז זייער הויך.

Where is the fire extinguisher?
vu iz der feyerlesher?
וואו איז דער פּייערלעשער?

There is a fire. I must call for help.
Do iz a fayer. ikh muz rufn hilf.
דאָ איז אַ פּייַער. איך מוז רופן הילף.

Fire hydrant - feyer plump פייער פלומפ
Fireman - feyerman פייערמאן
Emergency situation - noytfal situatsye נויטפאל סיטואציע
Explosion - ofrayzung אויפֿרײַסונג
Rescue - htslh הצלה
Natural disaster - natirlekh umglik נאטירלעכער אומגליק
Destruction - tseshterung צעשטערונג
Damage - shadn שאדן
Hurricane - hurrikan הוריקאַן
Tornado - Tornado טאָרנאַדאָ
Flood - mbul
Disaster - aumglik אומגליק
Disaster area - aumglik gegnt אומגליק געגנט
Mandatory - mandatori מאַנדאַטאָרי
Evacuation - evakuatsye עוואַקואַציע

It's prohibited to park by the fire in case of a fire.
es iz farvert tsu parkiren bey di fayer kheydrant in fal fun a fayer.
עס איז פֿאַרווערט צו פּאַרקירען בײַ די פּייַער פּלומפ אין פֿאַל פון אַ פּייַער

When there is a fire, the first to arrive on scene are the firemen.
ven es iz do a fayer, zenen di ershte angekumen aoyf der stsene di feyerlesher.
ווען עס איז דאָ אַ פּייער, זענען די ערשטע אנגעקומען אויף דער סצענע די פּייערלעשער.

In an emergency situation everyone needs to be rescued.
in a noytfal situatsye alemen darf vern geratevet.
אין אַ נויטפֿאַל סיטואַציע אַלעמען דאַרף ווערן געראַטעוועט.

The gas explosion led to a natural disaster.
di gaz ufraysung hat gefirt tsu a natirlekh umglik.
די גאַז אויפֿרײַסונג האָט געפֿירט צו אַ נאַטירלעך אומגליק.

During a siren you need to run to the bomb shelter.
beshas a siren ir darft loyfn tsu di bombe bashitsn.
בשעת סירען איר דאַרפֿט לויפֿן צו די באָמבע באַשיצן

This is a disaster area, therefore there is a mandatory evacuation order.
dos iz a umglik gegnt, deriber es iz a mandatori evakuatsye sdr.
דאָס איז אַן ומגליק געגנט, דעריבער עס איז דאָ אַ מאַנדאַטאָרי עוואַקואַציע סדר.

Overflow (water) - iberfleytsung איבערפֿלייצונג
Storm - shturem שטורעם
Snowstorm - shney shturem שניי שטורעם
Hail - hogl האָגל
Bomb shelter - bombe bashitsn באָמבע באַשיצן
Refuge - mklt מקלט
Cause - sibh סיבה
Safety - zikherkayt זיכערקייט
Drought - trikenish טריקעניש
Famine - hunger הונגער
Poverty - oremkayt אָרעמקייט
Epidemic - epidemye עפּידעמיע
Pandemic - pandemik פּאַנדעמיק
Earthquake - erdtsiternish ערדציטערניש

The hurricane caused a lot of damage and destruction in its path.
der harikein hat faraurzakht asakh shadns aun farnikhtung aoyf zeyn veg.
דער האַריקעין האָט פֿאַראורזאַכט אסאך שאדנס און פארניכטונג אויף זיין וועג.

The tornado destroyed the town.
di tornado hot khruv gemakht di shtot.
די טאָרנאַדאָ האָט חרוב געמאַכט די שטאָט.

The drought led to famine and a lot of poverty.
d i trikenish n hab n gefir t tsu m hunger, au n a s kh aremkeyt.
ך אַרעמקייט די טריקעניש האָט געפֿירט צום הונגער, און אס.

There were three days of flooding following the storm.
es zenen geven drey teg fun farfleytsung nakh dem shturem.
עס זענען געווען דריי טעג פֿון פֿאַרפֿלייצונג נאָך דעם שטורעם.

This is a snowstorm and not a hail storm.
das iz a shney-shturem aun nisht keyn hagl shturem.
דאָס איז אַ שניי-שטורעם און נישט קיין האָגל שטורעם.

We need to stay in a safe place during the earthquake.
mir darfn blaybn in a zikher ort beshas di erdtsiternish.
מיר דאַרפֿן בלייבן אין אַ זיכער אָרט בשעת די ערדציטערניש

Danger - gefahr געפֿאָר
Dangerous - geferlekh געפערלעך
A warning - a varenung א וואַרענונג
Warning! - varenung! וואַרענונג
Safe place - zikher ort זיכער אָרט
Blackout - blakaut בלאַקאָוט
Rainstorm - regnshturm רעגנשטורם
Avalanche - lavine לאַווינע
Heatwave - hits היץ
Rip current - rip kurant ריפ קוראַנט
Tsunami - Tsunami צונאַמי
Whirlpool - verlful ווערלפול
Lightning - blits בליץ
Thunder - duner דונער

There was a blackout for three hours due to the rainstorm.
es iz geven a blakaut far drey sheh rekht tsu der regn shturem.
עס איז געווען אַ בלאַקאָוט פֿאַר דריי שעה רעכט צו דער רעגן שטורעם.

Be careful during the snowstorm, because there might be an avalanche.
zey opgehit beshas di shney shturem, vayl es ken zeyn a lavine.
זיי אָפּגעהיט בשעת די שניי שטורעם, ווייַל עס קען זיין אַ לאַווינע.

There is no tsunami warning.
kh'hab nisht keyn tsunami-varenung.
כ'האב נישט קיין צונאמי-וואַרענונג.

You can't swim against a rip current.
ir kenen nisht shvimen kegn a rip kurant.
איר קענט נישט שווימען קעגן אַ ריפ קראַנט.

There is a risk of lightning today.
es iz a rizikirn fun blitsn haynt.
עס איז אַ ריזיקירן פון בליצן היינט.

Heatwaves are usually in the summer.
hitzen zenen geveyntlekh in di zumer.
היצן זענען געוויינטלעך אין די זומער.

HOME - HEYM היים

Living room - voyntsimer וווינציצער
Couch - sofe סאָפע / **Sofa** - divan סאָפע
Door - tir טיר / **Closet** - shafe שאַפע
Stairway - trep טרעפ
Rug - tepekh טעפעך
Curtain - forhang פֿאָרהאַנג
Window - fenster פענסטער
Floor - padloge פּאַדלאָגע / **Floor** (as in level) - shtok שטאָק

The living room is missing a couch and a sofa.
in di lebedik tsimer felt a kanape un a divan.
אין די וווינצימער פעלט אַ קאַנאַפע און אַ דיוואַן.

I must buy a new door for my closet.
ikh muz koyfn a naye tir far mayn shafe.
איך מוז קויפן אַ נײַע טיר פֿאַר מײַן שאַפע.

The spiral staircase is beautiful.
di spiralish leyter iz sheyn.
די ספּיראַליש לײַטער איז שײן.

There aren't any curtains on the windows.
es zenen nisht do keyn furhang aoyf di fentster.
עס זענען נישט דאָ קיין פֿאָרהאַנג אויף די פֿענצטער.

I have a marble floor on the first floor and a wooden floor on the second floor.
ikh hobn a mirmlshteyn shtok aoyf der ershter shtok aun a vudan shtok aoyf di rge shtok.
איך האָב אַ מירמלשטיין פֿאַדלאָגע אויף דער ערשטער שטאָק און אַ האָלצענעם .
פֿאַדלאָגע אויף דער צווייטער שטאק

I can only light this candle now.
ikh ken nor itst ontsindn dos likht.
איך קען נאָר איצט אָנצינדן דאָס ליכט.

I can clean the floors today and then I want to arrange the closet.
ikh kenen reynikn di florz haynt aun demolt ikh viln tsu tsuleygn di shafe.
איך קען רייניקן די פֿאַדלאָגעס הײַנט און דערנאָך וויל איך אראַנזשירן דער שאַפע.

123

Silverware - zilbervarg זילבערוואַרג
Knife - meser מעסער
Spoon - lefl לעפֿל
Fork - gopl גאָפּל
Teaspoon - lefele לעפעלע
Kitchen - kikh קיך
A cup - a glezl אַ גלעזל
Mug - begl בעגל
Plate - teler טעלער
Bowl - shisl שיסל / **Little bowl** - shisele שיסעלע
Napkin - servetke סערוועטקע
Table - tish טיש
Placemat - plasmat פּלאַסמאַט
Fireplace - kamin קאַמין / **Chimney** - koymen קוימען
Candle - likht ליכט

The knives, spoons, teaspoons, and forks are inside the drawer in the kitchen.
di neyvz, spunz, tispunz aun forx zenen in di shuflod in der kikh.
די נייווז, ספּונז, טיספּונז און פֿאַרקס זענען ין די שופֿלאָד אין דער קיך.

There aren't enough cups, plates, and silverware on the table for everyone.
es zenen nisht genug teplekh, plates aun zilbervare aoyf di tish far alemen.
עס זענען נישט גענוג טעפּלעך, פּלאַטעס און זילבערוואַרע אויף די טיש פֿאַר אַלעמען.

The napkin is underneath the bowl.
di servetke iz aunter di shisl.
די סערוועטקע איז אונטער די שיסל.

The placemats are on the table.
di plates zenen aoyf di tish.
די פּלאַטעס זענען אויף די טיש.

The fire sparkles in the fireplace.
dos fayer finklt in kamin.
דאָס פֿייער פֿינקלט אין קאַמין.

Tablecloth - tish tukh טיש טוך
Glass (material) - glaz גלאז
A glass (cup) - tepl טעפל
Oven - aoyvn אויוון
Stove - hrube הרובע
Pot (cooking) - top טאָפּ
Pan - Pan פּאַן
Shelve - politse פּאָליצע
Cabinet - kabinet קאַבינעט
Pantry - shpeyz שפּייז
Drawer - shuflod שופלאָד

The tablecloth is beautiful.
di tish tukh iz sheyn.
די טישטוך איז שיין.

There is canned food in the pantry.
es iz do pushkesin di shpayzkamer.
עס איז דאָ פּושקעס אין די שפּייזקאַמער.

Where are the toothpicks?
vau zenen di tseynshtekn?
וואו זענען די ציינשטעקן?

The glasses on the shelf are used for champagne, not wine.
di briln aoyf di politse zenen genitst far shampanyer, nisht veyn.
די ברילן אויף די פּאָליצע זענען געניצט פאַר שאַמפּאַניער, נישט ווייַן.

The pizza is in the oven.
der pitsa iz in di oyvn.
דער פּיצאַ איז אין די אויוון

The pots and pans are in the cabinet.
di tep aun skovrodes zenen in di kabinet.
די טעפּ און סקאָוואָראָדעס זענען אין די קאַבינעט.

The stove isn't functioning.
der hrube arbet nisht
דער הרובע ארבּעט נישט

Bedroom - shloftsimer שלאָפצימער
Bed - bet בעט
Mattress - matras מאַטראַטס
Blanket - fardekn פֿאַרדעקן / **Bedsheet** – laylech ליילעך
Pillow - kishn קישן
Mirror - shpigl שפּיגל
Chair - shtul שטול
Dining room - estsimer עסצימער
Hallway – koridor קאָרידאָר
Downstairs - auntn אונטן
Laundry detergent - vesh vashpulver וועש וואַשפּולווער
Trash - opfal אָפּפֿאַל / **Garbage can** - mist kastn מיסט קאַסטן

The master bedroom is at the end of the hallway, and the dining room is downstairs.
der hoipt shloftsimer iz in suf fun der koridor, aun di estsimer iz unten.
דער הױפּט שלאָפצימער איז אין סוף פֿון דער קאָרידאָר, און די עסצימער איז אונטן.

The mirror looks good in the bedroom.
der shpigl kukt ois gut in dem shloftsimer.
דער שפּיגל קוקט אױס גוט אין דעם שלאָפצימער.

I have to buy a new bed and a new mattress.
ikh muz koyfn a nay bet un a nay matras.
איך מוז קױפֿן אַ נײַ בעט און אַ נײַ מאַטראַטס.

Where are the blankets and bed sheets?
vu zenen di ferdeken aun di leilecher?
ווו זענען די פֿאַרדעקן און ליילעכער?

My pillows are on the chair.
meyne kishns zenen aoyf der shtul.
מײַנע קישנס זענען אױף דער שטול.

The garbage can is blocking the driveway.
di mist kasten farshtelt di araynfor.
די מיסט קאַסטן פֿאַרשטעלט די אַרײַנפֿאָר

I have to wash the rug with laundry detergent.
ikh muz vashn di tepekh mit vesh vashpulver.
איך מוז וואַשן די טעפּעך מיט וועש וואַשפּולווער

Towel - hantekh האַנטעך
Bathroom - klozet קלאָזעט
Bathtub - vane וואַנע
Shower - shprits שפריץ
Sink - zinken אפגאס
Faucet - kram קראָם
Soap - zeyf זייף
Bag - tash טאַש
Box - kestl קעסטל
Key - shlisl שליסל

These towels are for drying your hand.
di hantikher zenen far trikenen deyn hant.
די האַנטיכער זענען פֿאַר טריקענען דייַן האַנט

The bathtub, shower, and the sink are old.
di vane, shprits, aun di opgos zenen alt.
די וואַנע, שפריץ, און די אפגאס זענען אַלט.

I need soap to wash my hands.
ikh darf zeyf tsu vashn di hent.
איך דאַרף זייף צו וואַשן די הענט.

The guest bathroom is in the corner of the hallway.
di gast klozet iz in di vinkl fun di kholvey.
די גאַסט קלאָזעט איז אין די ווינקל פון די קארידאר

How many boxes does he have?
vi file kestlekh hat er?
?וו`פיל קעסטלעך האט ער

I want to put my things in the plastic bag.
ikh viln leygn meyn zakhn in di plastik zekl.
איך ווילן לייגן מײַנע זאכן אין די פלאַסטיק זעקל.

I need to bring my keys.
ikh darf brengen mayne shlislen.
איך דאַרף ברענגען מײַנע שליסלען.

127

Room - tsimer צימער
Balcony - balkon באַלקאָן
Roof - dakh דאַך
Ceiling - stelye סטעליע
Wall - vant וואַנט
Carpet - tepekh טעפּעך
Attic - boydem בוידעם
Basement - keler קעלער
Driveway – areinfuhr אַרייַנפאָר
Garden - gortn גאָרטן
Backyard – hoif הויף
Jar – sloiye סלויע
Doormat – tirmateh טיר מאַטע

I can install new windows for my balcony.
ikh kenen instalirn nay fentster far meyn balkon.
.איך קען אינסטאַלירן נייַ פֿענצטער פֿאַר מיין באַלקאָן

I must install a new roof.
ikh muz instalirn a nay dakh.
.איך מוז אינסטאַלירן אַ נייַ דאַך

The color of my ceiling is white.
di kolir fun meyn stelye iz vays.
.די קאָליר פֿון מיין סטעליע איז ווייַס

I must paint the walls.
ikh muz moln di vent.
.איך מוז מאָלן די וועענט

The attic is an extra room in the house.
di boydem iz an extre tsimer in di hoyz.
.די בוידעם איז אַן עקסטרע צימער אין די הויז

The kids are playing either in the basement or the backyard.
di kinder shpielen oder in di keler oder di hoif.
די קינדער שפילן אָדער אין די קעלער אָדער די הויף

All the glass jars are outside on the doormat.
ale di glezerne sloyes zenen in droisen aoyf di tir mat.
אלע די גלעזערנע סלויעס זענען אין דרויסן אויף די טיר מאַט

Conclusion

You have now learned a wide range of sentences in relation to a variety of topics such as the home and garden. You can discuss the roof and ceiling of a house, plus natural disasters like hurricanes and thunderstorms.

The combination of sentences can also work well when caught in a natural disaster and having to deal with emergency issues. When the electricity gets cut you can tell your family or friends, "I can only light this candle now." As you're running out of the house, remind yourself of the essentials by saying, "I need to bring my keys with me."

If you need to go to a hospital, you have now been provided with sentences and the vocabulary for talking to doctors and nurses and dealing with surgery and health issues. Most importantly, you can ask, "What is the emergency number in this country?" When you get to the hospital, tell the health services, "The hurricane caused a lot of destruction and damage in its path," and "We used the hurricane shelter for refuge."

The three hundred and fifty words that you learned in part 1 should have been a big help to you with these new themes. When learning the Yiddish language, you are now more able to engage with people in Yiddish, which should make your travels flow a lot easier.

Part 3 will introduce you to additional topics that will be invaluable to your journeys. You will learn vocabulary in relation to politics, the military, and the family. The three books in this series all together provide a flawless system of learning the Yiddish language.

When you proceed to Part 3 you will be able to expand your vocabulary and conversational skills even further. Your range of topics will expand to the office environment, business negotiations and even school.

Please, feel free to post a review in order to share your experience or suggest feedback as to how this method can be improved.

Conversational
Yiddish
Quick and Easy
The Most Innovative Technique
to Learn the Yiddish Language

Part III

YATIR NITZANY

Introduction to the Program

You have now reached Part 3 of Conversational Yiddish Quick and Easy. In Part 1 you learned the 350 words that could be used in an infinite number of combinations. In Part 2 you moved on to putting these words into sentences. You learned how to ask for help when your house was hit by a hurricane and how to find the emergency services. For example, if you need to go to a hospital, you have now been provided with sentences and the vocabulary for talking to doctors and nurses and dealing with surgery and health issues. When you get to the hospital, you can tell the health services, "The hurricane caused a lot of destruction and damage in its path," and "We used the hurricane shelter for refuge."

In this third book in the series, you will find the culmination of this foreign language course that is based on a system using key phrases used in day-to-day life. You can now move on to further topics such as things you would say in an office. This theme is ideal if you've just moved to Yiddish for a new job. You may be about to sit at your desk to do an important task assigned to you by your boss but you have forgotten the details you were given. Turn to your colleagues and say, "I have to write an important email but I forgot my password." Then, if the reply is "Our secretary isn't here today. Only the receptionist is here but she is in the bathroom," you'll know what is being said and you can wait for help. By the end of the first few weeks, you'll have at your disposal terminology that can help reflect your experiences. "I want to retire already," you may find yourself saying at coffee break on a Monday morning after having had to go to your bank manager and say, "I need a small loan in order to pay my mortgage this month."

I came up with the idea of this unique system of learning foreign languages as I was struggling with my own attempt to learn Yiddish. When playing around with word combinations I discovered 350 words that when used together could make up an infinite number of sentences. From this beginning, I was able to start speaking in a new language. I then practiced and found that I could use the same technique with other languages, such as Spanish, French, Italian and Arabic. It was a revelation.

This method is by far the easiest and quickest way to master other languages and begin practicing conversational language skills.

The range of topics and the core vocabulary are the main components of this flawless learning method. In Part 3 you have a chance to learn how to relate to people in many more ways. Sports, for example, are very important for keeping healthy and in good spirits. The social component of these types of activities should not be underestimated at all. You will, therefore, have much help when you meet some new people, perhaps in a bar, and want to say to them, "I like to watch basketball games," and "Today are the finals of the Olympic Games. Let's see who wins the World Cup."

For sports, the office, and for school, some parts of conversation are essential. What happens when you need to get to work but don't have any clean clothes to wear because of malfunctions with the machinery. What you need is to be able to pick up the phone and ask a professional or a friend, "My washing machine and dryer are broken so maybe I can wash my laundry at the public laundromat." When you finally head out after work for some drinks and meet a nice new man, you can say, "You can leave me a voicemail or send me a text message."

Hopefully, these examples help show you how reading all three parts of this series in combination will prepare you for all you need in order to boost your conversational learning skills and engage with others in your newly learned language. The first two books have been an important start. This third book adds additional vocabulary and will provide the comprehensive knowledge required.

OFFICE – byuro ביורָא

Boss – bal-habos בעל־הבית
Employee(s) - ongeshtelter אָנגעשטעלטער
Staff - arbeters אַרבעטערס
Meeting - zistung זיצונג
Conference room - konferents tsimer קאָנפֿערענץ צימער
Secretary - sekretar סעקרעטאַר
Receptionist - ufnemer אויפֿנעמער
Schedule - plan פּלאַן
Calendar - kalendar קאַלענדאַר

My boss asked me to give her the paperwork.
meyn balebas hat mikh gebetn ir tsu gebn di papiren.
מיין באלעבאס האט מיך געבעטן איר צו געבן די פאפירן.

Our secretary isn't here today. The receptionist is here but she is in the bathroom.
aundzer sekretar iz nisht do haynt. di ufnemerin iz do ober zi iz in vashtsimer.
אונדזער סעקרעטאַר איז נישט דאָ היינַט. די אויפֿנעמערין איז דאָ אָבער זי איז אין וואַשצימער.

The employee meeting can take place in the conference room.
di ongeshtelter bagegenish kenen nemen ort in di konferents tsimer.
די אָנגעשטעלטער באַגעגעניש קען נעמען אָרט אין די קאָנפֿערענץ צימער.

My business cards are inside my briefcase.
mayne gesheft kartlekh zenen in meyn teke.
מיַינע געשעפט קאַרטלעך זענען אין מיין טעקע.

The office staff must check their work schedule daily.
di byuro arbeters muzn kontrolirn zeyer arbet plan teglekh.
די ביורָא אַרבעטערס מוזן קאָנטראָלירן זייער אַרבעט פּלאַן טעגלעך.

Supplies – zapas זאפאס
Pencil - blayer בלייער
Pen - feder פעדער
Ink - tint טינט
Eraser - meker מעקער
Desk - shraybtish שרייבטיש
Cubicle – alker אלקער
Chair - shtul שטול
Office furniture - byuro mebl ביוראָ מעבל
Business card - gesheft kort געשעפֿטקאָרט
Lunch break – mitog hafsoke מיטאָג הפֿסקה
Days off - freye teg פֿרייע טעג
Briefcase - teke טעקע
Bathroom - vashtsimer וואַשצימער

I am going to buy office furniture.
ikh gey koyfn byuro mebl.
איך גיי קויפֿן ביוראָ מעבל.

There isn't any ink in this pen.
es iz nisht do keyn tint in dem feder.
עס איז נישט דאָ קיין טינט אין דעם פעדער.

This pencil is missing an eraser.
dem blayer hot nisht keynmeker.
די בלייער האָט נישט קיין מעקער.

Our days off are written on the calendar.
aunzere freye teg vern geshribn aoyfn kalendar.
אונזערע פֿרייע טעג ווערן געשריבן אויפֿן קאַלענדאַר.

I need to buy extra office supplies.
ikh darf koyfn iberike ofis zapas.
איך דאַרף קויפֿן איבעריקע אָפֿיס זאפאס.

I am busy until my lunch break.
ikh bin farnumen biz meyn mitog hafsoke.
איך בין פאַרנומען ביז מיין מיטאָג הפֿסקה

Laptop - shoys komputer שויס קאָמפּוטער
Computer - komputer קאָמפּוטער
Keyboard - klavyatur קלאַוויאַטור
Mouse - mayzl מײַזל
Email - blitspost בליצפּאָסט
Password - parol פּאַראָל
Attachment - tsulog צולאָג
Printer - druker דרוקער
Colored printer - kolirte druker קאָלירטע דרוקער

I want to write an important email but I forgot my password for my account.
ikh vil shraybn a vikhtike blitspost ober ikh hob fargesn meyn parol far meyn konte.
איך וויל שרײַבן אַ וויכטיקע בליצפּאָסט אָבער איך האָב פֿאַרגעסן מיין פּאַראָל פֿאַר מיין קאָנטע.

I need to purchase a computer, a keyboard, a printer, and a desk.
ikh darf koyfn a kompiuter, a klavyatur, a druker aun a shraybtish.
איך דאַרף קויפֿן אַ קאָמפּיוטער, אַ קלאַוויאַטור, אַ דרוקער און אַ שרײַבטיש.

Where is the mouse on my laptop?
vu iz dos mayzl aoyf meyn shoyskomputer?
וווּ איז דאָס מײַזל אויף מיין שויסקאָמפּיוטער?

Do you have a colored printer?
Hot ir a kolirt druker?
האָט איר אַ קאָלירט דרוקער?

I needed to fax the contract but instead, I decided to send it as an attachment in the email.
ikh darf faksn dem kontrakt ober anshtot dem hob ikh bashlosn tsu shikn es vi a tsulog in dem blitsbriv.
איך דאַרף פֿאַקסן דעם קאָנטראַקט אָבער אנשטאָט דעם האָב איך באַשלאָסן צו שיקן עס ווי אַ צולאָג אין דעם בליצבריוו.

To download - tsu aroplodn צו אַראָבלאָדן
To upload - tsu aruflodn צו אַרויפֿלאָדן
Internet - Internets אינטערנעץ
Account - khshbun קאָנטע
A copy - a kopye אַ קאָפּיע
To copy - tsu kopirn צו קאָפּירן
Paste - pap פּאַפּ
Fax - Fax פֿאַקס
Scanner - skanirer סקאָנירער
To scan - tsu skanirn צו סקאָנירן
Telephone - telefon טעלעפֿאָן
Charger - tsharjer טשאַרדזשער
To charge (a phone) - tsu tsharjen צו טשאַרדזשען

The internet is slow today therefore it's difficult to upload or download.
der internets iz pamelekh haynt, deriber es iz shver tsu aruflodn oder aroplodn.
דער אינטערנעץ איז פּאַמעלעך היַנט, איז עס איז שווער צו אַרויפֿלאָדן אָדער אַראָפֿלאָדן.

One day, the fax machine will be completely obsolete.
A mol vet der faks mashin vet zeyn engansn fareltert.
אַ מאָל וועט די פֿאַקס מאַשין זיַין אינגאַנסן פֿאַרעלטערט.

Where is my phone charger?
vu iz meyn telefon tsharjer?
ווו איז מיַין טעלעפֿאָן טשאַרדזשער?

The scanner is broken.
der skanner iz tsebrokhn.
דער סקאָננער איז צעבראַכן.

The telephone is behind the chair.
der telefon iz hinter dem shtul.
דער טעלעפֿאָן איז הינטער דעם שטול.

Shredder - shreder שרעדער
Copy machine - kopi mashin קאָפּי מאַשין
Filing cabinet - dosiye kabinet דאָסיע קאַבינעט
Paper - papir פּאַפּיר, **(p)** tseytungen צייטונגען
Page - blat בלאַט, (p) bleter בלעטער
Paperwork - peyperverk פּייפּערווערק
Portfolio - portfel פּאָרטפעל
Files - tekes טעקעס
Document - dokument דאָקומענט
Deadline - termin טערמין

The copy machine is next to the telephone.
di kopye mashin iz lebn di telefon.
די קאָפּיע מאַשין איז לעבן די טעלעפֿאָן.

I can't find my stapler, paper clips, nor my highlighter in my cubicle.
ikh ken nisht gefinen meyn stapler, klemerlech, oder meyn hoichpunkt in meyn kabinet.
איך קען נישט געפֿינען מיין סטאַפּלער, קלעמערלעך, אָדער מיין הויכפּונקט אין .
מיין קאַבינעט

The filing cabinet is full of documents.
di filing kabinet iz ful mit dokumentn.
דער דאָסיע קאַבינעט איז פֿול מיט דאָקומענטן

The garbage can is full.
Dos mist kestl iz ful.
דאָס מיסט קעסטל איז פֿול.

Give me the file because today is the deadline.
gebn mir di teke vayl haynt iz di termin.
געב מיר די טעקע ווייַל היַינט איז די טערמין.

Contract - kontrakt קאָנטראַקט
Records - rekords רעקאָרדס
Archives - artkhives אַרכיוועס
Binder - binder בינדער
Paper clip - klemerl קלעמערל
Stapler - stefler סטעפלער
Staples - stefles סטעפלעס
Stamp - shtempl שטעמפּל
Mail - Post פּאָסט
Letter - briv בריוו
Envelope - konvert קאָנווערט
Data - Data דאַטן
Analysis - analisis אַנאַליסיס
Highlighter – hoykhpunkt הויכפּונקט
Marker - marker מאַרקער
To highlight – aroishayben אַרויסהייבן
Ruler - vire ווירע

The supervisor at our company is responsible for data analysis.
der mashgyekh in aundzer firme iz farantvortlekh far datn analisis.
דער משגיח אין אונדזער פירמע איז פאַראַנטוואָרטלעך פֿאַר דאַטן אַנאַליסיס.

Where do I put the binder?
vu zol ikh shteln di binder?
ווו זאָל איך שטעלן די בינדער?

The ruler is next to the shredder.
der hersher iz nebn der shreder.
דער הערשער איז נעבן דער שרעדער.

I need a stamp and an envelope.
ikh darf a shtempl aun a konvert.
איך דאַרף אַ שטעמפּל און אַ קאָנווערט.

There is a letter in the mail.
es iz a briv in di post.
עס איז אַ בריוו אין די פּאָסט.

SCHOOL - SHULE שולע

Student - talmid תּלמיד
Teacher - lerer לערער
Substitute teacher – vertreiter פֿאַרטרעטער
A class - a klas אַ קלאַס
A classroom - a klastsimer אַ קלאַסצימער
Education - dertsiung דערצִיונג

The classroom is empty.
di klastsimer iz leydik.
.די קלאַסצימער איז ליידיק

I want to bring my laptop to class.
ikh vil brengen meyn laptap tsu klas.
.איך וויל ברענגען מיין לאַפּטאַפּ צו קלאַס

Our math teacher is absent and therefore a substitute teacher replaced him.
aundzer matematik lerer iz nito aun deriber a fartreter lerer ripleyst im.
.אונדזער מאַטעמאַטיק לערער איז ניטאָ און דעריבער אַ פֿאַרטרעטער פֿאַרבייט אים

All the students are present.
ale studentn zenen do.
.אַלע סטודענטן זענען דאָ

Make sure to pass your classes because you can't fail this semester.
makh zikher durchmachen deyn klasn vayl ir kenen nisht farlozn dem semester
מאַך זיכער דארכמאכן דיין קלאַסן ווייַל איר קענט נישט דורכפֿאַלן דעם .
סעמעסטער

The education level at a private school is much more intense.
der bildung mdrgh in a privat shule iz fil mer tif.
.דער בילדונג מדרגה אין אַ פּריוואַט שולע איז פיל מער טיף

Private school - private shule פּריוואַטע שולע
Public school - folksshule פֿאָלקסשולע
Elementary school - elementar shule עלעמענטאַר שולע
Middle school - mitlshul מיטלשול
High school - mitlshul מיטלשול
University - auniversitet אוניווערסיטעט
College - kolege קאָלעגע
Grade (level) - klas קלאַס
Grade (grade on a test) - grade גראַדע
Pass – durchmachen דורכמאַכן
Fail - durkhfal דורכפֿאַל
Absent - nito ניטאָ
Present – itztig איצטיג

I went to a public elementary and middle school.
ikh bin gegangen tsu a folks elementar aun mitl shule.
איך בין געגאַנגען צו אַ פֿאָלקס עלעמענטאַר און מיטל שולע.

I have good memories of high school.
ikh hab gute zkhrunus fun mitlshul.
איך האב גוטע זכרונות פֿון מיטלשול.

My son is 15 years old and he is in the ninth grade.
mayn zun iz 15 yor alt aun er iz in di naynte klas.
מײַן זון איז 15 יאָר אַלט און ער איז אין די נײַנטע קלאַס.

You must get good grades on your report card.
du muzt bakumen gute grades aoyf deyn barikht kartl.
דו מוזט באַקומען גוטע גראַדעס אויף דײַן באַריכט קאַרטל.

College textbooks are expensive.
kolege textbux zenen tayer.
קאָלעגע לערנביכער זענען טײַער.

I want to study at an out-of-state university.
ikh villernen in an aoys-fun-shtat auniversitet.
איך וויל לערנען אין אַן אויס-פֿון-שטאַט אוניווערסיטעט.

Backpack - bakpak באקפּאק
Notebook - heft העפֿט
Subject - enin ענין
Science - visnshaft וויסנשאַפֿט
Chemistry - khemye כעמיע
Physics - fizik פֿיזיק
Geography - geografye געאָגראַפֿיע
History - geshikhte געשיכטע
Math - matematik מאַטעמאַטיק
Addition – chibur חיבּור
Subtraction - khiser חיסור
Division – teilung טיילונג
Multiplication - multiplikatsye מולטיפּליקאַציע

At school, geography is my favorite class, English is easy, math is hard, and history is boring.
in shule, geografi iz meyn balibste klas, english iz gring, mat iz shver, aun geshikhte iz nudne.
אין שולע, געאָגראַפֿי איז מײַן באַליבסטע קלאַס, ענגליש איז גרינג, מאַט איז שווער, און געשיכטע איז נודנע.

After English class, there is physical education.
nokh english klas, iz do gimnastik
נאָך ענגליש קלאַס, איז דא גימנאַסטיק.

Today's math lesson is on addition and subtraction. Next month it will be division and multiplication.
di heyntike matematik lektsye iz aoyf khibur aun khiser. Neksten khodesh vet zeyn fun obteil un mulitplikatsye.
די הײַנטיגע מאַטעמאַטיק לעקציע איז אויף חיבּור און חיסור. נעקסטן חודש וועט זײַן אויף טיילונג און מולטיפּליקאַציע

The teacher wants to teach the students roman numerals.
der lerer vil lernen di studentn roymer numerals.
דער לערער וויל לערנען די סטודענטן רוימער נומעראַלס.

I think my notebook and calculator are in my backpack.
ikh denk az meyn heft un kalkulator zenen in meyn bakpak.
איך דענק אז מײַן העפֿט און קאַלקולאַטאָר זענען אין מײַן באַקפּאַק.

Language - shprakh שפּראַך
English - english ענגליש
Foreign language - fremd shprakh פרעמד שפּראַך
Physical education – gimnastik גימנאַסטיק
Chalk - krayd קרײַד
Board – tovel טאָוול
Report card - barikht kartl באַריכט קאַרטל
Alphabet - alfabet אלפאבעט
Letters - osyos אותיות
Words - verter ווערטער
To review - uberkuken אובערקוקן
Dictionary - verterbukh ווערטערבוך
Detention - farhaltung פאַרהאַלטונג
The principle - der printsipal דער פרינציפּאַל

This year for foreign language credits, I want to choose Spanish and French.
dem yor far fremd shprakh kredits, vil ich klaybn shpanish aun frantsoyzish.
דעם יאָר פֿאַר פרעמד שפּראַך קרעדיטס וויל איך קלײַבן שפּאַניש און פראַנצוייש.

I want to buy a dictionary, thesaurus, and a journal for school.
ikh vill koyfn a verterbukh, tesaurus aun a zhurnal far shule.
איך קויפן אַ ווערטערבוך, טעסאַורוס און אַ זשורנאַל פֿאַר שולע.

The teacher needs to write the homework on the board with chalk.
der lerer darf shraybn di lektsyes aoyf di bret mit krayd.
דער לערער דאַרף שרײַבן די לעקציעס אויף דעם טאָוול מיט קרײַד.

Today the students have to review the letters of the alphabet.
heynt darfn di studentn iberkukn di ausius funem alfabet.
היינט דאַרפן די סטודענטן איבערקוקן די אותיות פונעם אלפאבעט.

If you can't behave well then you must go to the principal's office, and maybe stay after school for detention.
aoyb ir kent zich nisht gut oiffiren, mizt ir geyn tsum printsipal's buro, aun afshr blaybn nokh sof shule far farhaltung.
אויב איר קענט זיך נישט גוט אויפפירן מוזט איר גיין צום פרינציפּאַלס בוירא, און אפֿשר בלײַבן נאָך סוף שולע פאר פערהאַלטונג

Test - Test טעסט
Quiz - oysfreg אויספרעג
Lesson - lektsye לעקציע
Notes – notitzn נאטיצן
Homework - lektsyes לעקציעס
Assignment - oifgabe אויפגאבע
Project - proyekt פּראָיעקט
Crayons - kraydl קרײַדל
Lunchbox - lontsh kestl לאָנטש קעסטל
Glue - kley קלײַ
Scissors - sher שער

Today, we don't have a test but we have a surprise quiz.
Haynt hobn mir nisht a probe ober mir hobn an umgerichte oysfreg.
היינט האָבן מיר נישט קיין טעסט אָבער מיר האָבן אן אומגעריכטע אויספרעג

Are a pen, a pencil, and an eraser included with the school supplies?
zenen a feder, a blayer aun a meker arayngerekhnt mit di shule sapleyz?
זענען אַ פעדער, אַ בלײַער און אַ מעקער אריינגערעכנט מיט די שולע סאַפלייז?

I need glue and scissors for my project.
ikh darfn kley aun a sher far meyn proyekt.
איך דאַרף קלײַ און אַ שער פֿאַר מיין פרויעקט.

I need tape and a stapler to fix my book.
ikh darf teyp aun a heftler tsu farrikhtn meyn bukh.
איך דאַרף טייף און אַ העפטלער צו פֿאַררירכטן מיין בוך.

You have to concentrate in order to take notes.
ir darft kansantriren tsu nemen notitzen
איר דארפט קאָנסאָנטרירן צו נעמען נאטיצן.

I forgot my lunchbox and crayons at home.
ikh hob fargesn meyn lontsh kestl aun meine kreindlech in shtub.
איך האָב פֿאַרגעסן מיין לאָנטש קעסטל און קריינדלעך אין שטוב.

Book - bukh בוך
Folders - teke טעקע
Papers – papiren פּאַפּירן
Calculator - kalkulator קאַלקולאַטאָר
Adhesive tape - klepik teyp קלעפּיק טייפּ
Lunch - mitag מיטאָג / **Cafeteria** - kafeterye קאַפעטעריע
Kindergarten - kindergortn קינדערגאָרטן
Pre-school - priskul פּריסקול **Daycare** togheim טאָגהיים
Triangle – dreiek דרייעק
Square - kvadrat קוואַדראַט / **Circle** - krayz קרייַז

All my papers are in my folder.
ale meyn papieren zenen in meyn teke.
אַלע מיינע פּאַפּירן זענען אין מיין טעקע.

The school librarian wants to invite the art and music teacher to the library next week.
der shul-biblyotekarin vil farbetn dem kunst- aun muzik-lerer in der biblyotek kumendike vokh.
דער שול־ביבליאָטעקאַרין וויל פֿאַרבעטן דעם קונסט־ און מוזיק־לערער אין דער ביבליאָטעק קומענדיקע וואָך.

For lunch, your children can purchase food at the cafeteria or they can bring food from home.
Af mitog, deyn kinder kenen koyfn esnvarg in di kafeterye oder zey kenen brengen esnvarg fun shtub.
אויף מיטאָג, דיינע קינדער קענען קויפן עסנוואַרג אין די קאַפעטעריע אָדער זיי קענען ברענגען עסנוואַרג פון שטוב.

To draw shapes such as a triangle, square, circle, and rectangle is easy.
tsu tseychenen formen azoi vi a drayek, kvadrat, krayz aun grodek, iz gring.
צו צייכענען פֿאַרמען אַזוי ווי אַ דרייעק, קוואַדראַט, קרייַז און גראַדעק, איז גרינג.

During the week, my youngest child is at daycare, my middle one is in pre-school, and the oldest is in kindergarten.
in der vokh, meyn yingste kind iz in di kinderheim, meyn mitlste iz in pri-shule, aun di eltste iz in kindergortn.
אין דער וואָך, מיין יאָנגגאַסט קינד איז אין די קינדערהיים, מיין מיטל איז אין פּרי־שולע, און די אָלדאַסט איז אין קינדער - גאַרטן.

144

PROFESSION - FAKH פֿאַך

Doctor - doktor דאָקטאָר
Nurse – kranken shvester קראנקן שוועסטער
Psychologist - psikholog פּסיכאָלאָג
Psychiatrist - psikhyater פּסיכיאַטער
Veterinarian - veterinar וועטערינאַר
Lawyer - advokat אַדוואָקאַט
Judge - rikhter ריכטער
Pilot - Pilot פּילאָט
Flight attendant – stuardke סטטוארדקע

What's your profession?
vos iz deyn fakh?
וואָס איז דיין פֿאַך?

I am going to medical school to study medicine because I want to be a doctor.
ikh gey in meditsinish shule tsu lernen meditsin vayl ikh vil zeyn a dokter.
איך גיי אין מעדיציניש שולע צו לערנען מעדיצין ווייל איך וויל זיין אַ דאָקטער.

There is a difference between a psychologist and a psychiatrist.
es iz do a khiluk tsvishn a psikholog aun a psikhiater.
עס איז דאָ אַ חילוק צווישן אַ פּסיכאָלאָג און אַ פּסיכיאַטער.

Most children want to be an astronaut, a veterinarian, or an athlete.
ruv kinder viln zeyn an astronat, a veterinar oder an atlet.
רובֿ קינדער ווילן זיין אַן אַסטראָנאַוט, אַ וועטערינאַר אָדער אַן אַטלעט.

The judge spoke to the lawyer at the courthouse.
der rikhter hat geredt mitn advakat inem gerikht hoyz.
דער ריכטער האָט גערעדט מיטן אַדוואָקאַט אינעם געריכט הויז.

Are you a photographer?
zent ir a fotografist?
זענט איר אַ פֿאָטאָגראַפֿיסט?

The flight attendant and the pilot are on the plane.
di stuardke aun der pilot zenen aoyf dem eroplan
די סטוארדקעע און דער פּילאָט זענען אויף דעם עראפּלאן

145

Reporter - Reporter רעפּאָרטער
Journalist - zhurnalist זשורנאַליסט
Electrician - elektriker עלעקטריקער
Mechanic - mekhaniker מעכאַניקער
Investigator – forsher פֿאָרשער
Detective - detektiv דעטעקטיוו
Translator - iberzetser איבערזעצער
Producer - produtsirer פּראָדוצירער
Director - direktor דירעקטאָר

The police investigator needs to investigate this case.
der falitsey aoysfarsher darf aoysfarshn dem fal.
דער פּאָליציי אויספֿאַרשער דאַרף אויספֿאַרשן דעם פֿאַל.

Being a detective could be a fun job.
zeyn a detektiv ken zeyn a voile arbet.
זײַן אַ דעטעקטיוו קען זײַן אַ וווילע אַרבעט.

I am a certified electrician.
ikh bin a sertafeyd elektriker.
איך בין אַ סערטאַפֿייד עלעקטריקער.

The mechanic overcharged me.
der mekhaniker hot mikh ibergerekhent
דער מעכאַניקער האָט מיך איבערגערעכנט

I want to be a journalist.
ikh vil vern a zhurnalist.
איך וויל ווערן אַ זשורנאַליסט.

The best translators work at my company.
di bester iberzetser arbet in meyn firme.
די בעסטע איבערזעצערן אַרבעטן אין מײַן פֿירמע.

I want to find the directors of the company.
ikh vilgefinen di direktors fun di firme.
איך וויל געפֿינען די דירעקטאָרס פֿון די פֿירמע.

Artist (performer) - kinstler קינסטלער
Artist (draws paints picture) - kinstler קינסטלער
Author - mkhbr מחבר
Painter – moler מאלער
Dancer - tantser טנצער
Writer - shreyber שרייבער
Photographer - fotografist פֿאָטאָגראַפֿיסט
Cook - kukher קוכער / **A chef** - a shef אַ שעף
Waiter - kelner קעלנער
Bartender - barshenker באַרשענקער

The artist produced this artwork for her catalog.
di kinstler hat geshafn dem kinstverk far ir katalog.
די קינסטלער האט געשאפן דעם קינסטווערק פֿאַר איר קאַטאַלאָג .

The artist drew a sketch.
der kinstler hot getseylt a skitse.
דער קינסטלער האָט געמאלט א סקיצע.

I want to apply as a cook at the restaurant instead of as a waiter.
ikh vil zikh onvendn vi a kokhn in dem restoran anshtot vi a kelner.
איך וויל זיך אָנווענדן ווי אַ קאָכן אין דעם רעסטאָראַן אַנשטאָט ווי אַ קעלנער.

The gardener can only come on weekdays.
der gertner kan kumen nar in vakh-teg.
דער גערטנער קאָן קומען נאר אין וואַך־טעג.

I have to go to the barbershop now.
ikh muz itst geyn in der shererei.
איך מוז איצט גיין אין דער שערעריי.

Being a bartender isn't an easy job.
tsu zeyn a barshenker iz nisht an gring arbet.
צו זיין אַ באַרשענקער איז נישט א גרינג אַרבעט .

Barber shop – shererei שערעריי
Barber - sherer שערער
Stylist - stilist סטיליסט
Maid - dinst דינסט
Housekeeper - bel-hbiste בעל־הביתטע
Caretaker – oifze'er אויפזעער
Farmer - poyer פּויער
Gardner - Gardner גאַרדנער
Mailman – postman פּאסטמאן
A guard - a vekhter א וועכטער
A cashier - a kasirer א קאסירער

Why do we need another maid?
farvas darfn mir nakh a dinst?
פּארוואס דארפֿן מיר נאך א דינסט?

I want to file a complaint against the mailman.
ikh vil makhen a taine kegn der postman.
איך וויל מאכן א טענה קעגן דער פּאסטמאן.

I am a part-time artist.
ikh bin a teyl-tseyt kinstler.
איך בין אַ טייל-צייט קינסטלער.

She was a dancer at the play.
zi iz geven a tentserin in der pyese.
זי איז געווען אַ טענצערין אין דער פּיעסע.

You need to contact the insurance company if you want to find another caretaker.
ir darft kontakten di farzikherung gezelshaft aoyb ir vilt gefinen an andere oifze'er.
איר דארפֿט קאָנטאַקטן די פֿאַרזיכערונג געזעלשאַפּט אויב איר ווילט געפֿינען אן אנדערע אויפזעער

The farmer can sell us ripened tomatoes today.
der poyer kon aundz haynt farkoyfn reypene tamatn.
דער פּויער קאָן אונדז היַינט פֿאַרקויפֿן רייפּענע טאָמאַטן.

BUSINESS - GESHEFT געשעפט

A business - a gesheft א געשעפט
Company - firme פֿירמע
Factory - fabrik פֿאַבריק
A professional - a frafesyanal א פּראָפֿעסיאנאל
Position - shtele שטעלע
Work, job - arbet אַרבעט
Employee - ongeshtelter אָנגעשטעלטער
Owner - bazitser באַזיצער
Manager - farvalter פֿאַרוואַלטער
Management - farvaltung פֿאַרוואַלטונג
Secretary - sekretar סעקרעטאַר

I need a job.
ikh darf an arbet.
איך דאַרף אַן אַרבעט.

She is the secretary of the company.
zi iz di sekretarin fun der firme.
זי איז די סעקרעטאַרין פֿון דער פֿירמע.

The manager needs to hire another employee.
der farvalter darf onshteln an ander ongeshtelter.
דער פֿאַרוואַלטער דאַרף אָנשטעלן אן אנדער אָנגעשטעלטער.

I am lucky because I have an interview for a cashier position today.
der farvalter darf onshteln an ander ongeshtelter.
איך בין מאַזלדיק ווייַל איך האָב אַן אינטערוויו פֿאַר אַ קאַסירער שטעלע היינט.

How much is the salary and does it include benefits?
vi fil iz di getsolt aun tut es araynnemen benefitn?
וויפֿיל איז די געצאָלט און טוט עס אַרייַננעמען בענעפֿיטן?

Management has your resumé and they need to show it to the owner of the company.
farvaltung hat deyn nemen zikh vider aun zey darfn tsu vayzn es tsu di bazitser fun di firme.
דער פֿאַרוואַלטונג האָט דייַן רעזומע און זיי דאַרפֿן עס צו די באַזיצער פֿון די פֿירמע.

149

An interview - an interviu אַן אינטערוויו

Resumé - Resumé רעזומעי

Presentation - prezentirung פּרעזענטירונג

Specialist - mumkhe מומכע

To hire - tsu onshteln צו אָנשטעלן

To fire - tsu fayer צו פײַער

Paycheck - batsoln tshek באַצאָלן טשעק

Income - hakhnose האַכנאָסע

Salary - getsolt געצאָלט

Insurance - farzikherung פֿאַרזיכערונג

Benefits – benefitn בענעפֿיטן

Trimester - Trimester טרימעסטער

Budget - bujet בודזשעט

Net - Nets נעץ

Gross - grob גראָב

To retire - tsu penzioniren zikh צו פּענזיאָנירן זיך

Pension - pensye פּענסיע

I am at work at the factory now.
ikh bin itst in der arbet in der fabrik.
איך בין איצט אין דער אַרבעט אין דער פֿאַבריק.

In business, you should be professional.
in gesheft, zolt ir zaynfakhmanish.
אין געשעפֿט, זאָלט איר זײַן פֿאַכמאַניש.

Is the presentation ready?
iz di prezentirung greyt?
איז די פּרעזענטירונג גרייט?

The first trimester is part of the annual budget.
der ershter trimester iz teyl fun di yerlekh bujet.
דער ערשטער טרימעסטער איז טייל פֿון די יערלעך בודזשעט.

I have to see the net and gross profits of the business.
ikh muzn zen di nets aun grob prafits fun di gesheft.
איך מוז זען די נעץ און גראָב פּראָפֿיץ פֿון די געשעפֿט.

I want to retire already.
ikh vil zich shoyn pensioniren.
איך וויל זיך שוין פּענסיאָנירן

Client - klyent קליענט

Broker - mekler מעקלער

Salesperson - farkoyfer פֿאַרקויפֿער

Realtor - ryalter ריאַלטער

Real Estate Market - grunteygns market גרונטייגנס מאַרקעט

A purchase - a koyfn אַ קויפֿן

To invest - tsu investirn צו ינוועסטירן

Investment – investitsia אינוועסטיציע

Stock – aktzias אקציעס

Stockbroker - berze mekler בערזע מעקלער

I can earn a huge profit from stocks.
ikh ken fardinen a rizik nuts fun stax.
איך קען פֿאַרדינען אַ ריזיק נוץ פֿון סטאַקס.

The demand in the real estate market depends on the country's economy.
di foderung in di grunteygns mark vendt zich aoyf di medine's ekanomye.
די פֿאָדערונג אין די גרונטייגנס מאַרק ווענדט זיך אויף די מדינה'ס עקאנאמיע.

If you want to sell your home, I can recommend a very good realtor.
aoyb ir vilt farkoyfn ayer heym, ikh ken rekomendirn a zeyer guter ryalter.
אויב איר ווילט פֿאַרקויפֿן אייער היים, איך קען רעקאָמענדירן אַ זייער גוטער ריאַלטער.

The investor wants to invest in this shopping center because of its good potential.
der invester vil investirn in dem shoping tsenter vegen dem guten potentsyel.
דער אינוועסטער וויל אינוועסטירן אין דעם שאַפּינג צענטער וועגן דעם גוטן פּאָטענציעל.

The value of the property increased by twenty percent.
di vert fun der farmog iz gevaxn mit tsvantsik protsent.
די ווערט פֿון דער פֿאַרמאָג איז געוואָקסן מיט צוואַנציק פּראָצענט.

How much is the commission on the sale?
vi fil iz di komisye aoyf dem farkoyf?
ווי פֿיל איז די קאָמיסיע אויף דעם פֿאַרקויף?

A lease - a dingen א דינגען
To lease - tsu dingen צו דינגען
Landlord - bel hbis בעל הבית
Tenant - lokator לאָקאַטאָר
Economy - ekanamye עקאנאמיע
Mortgage - hipotek היפאָטעק
Interest rate - interes rates אינטערעס ראָטעס
A loan - a antlayen אַ אַנטלייַען
Commission - komisye קאָמיסיע
Percent - protsent פּראָצענט
A sale - a farkoyf אַ פאַרקויף
Value - vert ווערט
Profit - nuts נוץ
The demand - di foderung די פאָדערונג
The supply - di tsushteln די צושטעלן
A contract - a kontrakt אַ קאָנטראַקט
Terms - tnoim תּנאָים
Signature - khsime חתימה
Initials - initsyaln איניציאַלן

The client wants to lease instead of purchasing the property.
der klyent vil tsu dingen anshtot fun pertshasing di farmog.
דער קליענט וויל צו דינגען אַנשטאָט פון קויפן די פאַרמאָג.

What are the terms of the purchase?
vos zenen di terminen fun koyfn?
וואָס זענען די טערמינען פון קויפן?

I can negotiate a better interest rate.
ikh kenen farhandlen a beser interes.
איך קען פאַרהאַנדלען אַ בעסער אינטערעס.

I need a small loan in order to pay my mortgage this month.
ikh darf a kleyn antlayen tsu tsoln meyn hipotek dem khudsh.
איך דאַרף אַ קליין אַנטלייַען צו צאָלן מיין היפאָטעק דעם חודש.

I need a signature and initials on the contract.
ikh darf a khsime aun initsyaln aoyf dem kontrakt.
איך דאַרף אַ חתימה און איניציאַלן אויף דעם קאָנטראַקט

Money - gelt געלט
Currency - krantkayt קראנטקייט
Cash - gelt געלט
Coins – rendlech רענדלעך
Change (change for a bill) – veksel וועקסל
Credit - kredit קרעדיט
Tax - shteyer שטייער
Price - prayz פרייז
Invoice – faktur פאקטור
Merchandise - skhurh סחורה
A refund - a tsuriktsol א צוריקצאָל
Produced - geshafn געשאפן
Imports - araynfir אריינפיר
Exports - export עקספּאָרט

Don't forget to bring cash with you.
du zalst nisht fargesn tsu brengen gelt mit ir.
דו זאלסט נישט פארגעסן צו ברענגען געלט מיט איר.

Do you have change for a 100 Euro bill?
tsi hot ir enderungen far a 100 eyro rekhenung?
צי האָט איר וועקסל פֿאָר אַ 100 ייראָ רעכענונג?

I don't have a credit card.
ikh hob nisht a kredit kartl.
איך האָב נישט אַ קרעדיט קאַרטל.

The salesperson told me there is no refund.
der farkoyfer hot mir gezogt az es iz keyn tsuriktsol.
דער פאַרקויפער האָט מיר געזאָגט אַז עס איז קיין צוריקצאָל.

This product is produced in Italy.
der produkt iz geshafn in italye.
דער פּראָדוקט איז געשאפן אין איטאליע.

I work in the export/import business.
ikh arbet in di export / araynfir gesheft.
איך אַרבעט אין די עקספּאָרט /אַריינפיר געשעפט.

Retail - lakhodim לאַכאדים
Wholesale – hurt הורט
To ship - tsu shikn צו שיקן
Shipment - transport טראַנספּאָרט
Product - produkt פּראָדוקט
Inventory - invantar אינוואַנטאָר
Advertisement – reklame רעקלאַמע
To advertise - tsu reklamieren רעקלאַמירן

Let me check my inventory.
loz mir iberkiken meyn invantori.
לאָז מיר איבערקוקן מיין אינוואַנטאָרי.

This product is insured.
der produkt iz farzikhert.
דער פּראָדוקט איז פאַרזיכערט.

This invoice contains a mistake.
dem invoys kull a grayz.
דעם אינוווייס האַט אַ גרייז.

What is the wholesale and retail value of this shipment?
vos iz di hurt aun lakhodim vert fun dem transport?
וואָס איז די הורט און לאַכאַדים ווערט פון דעם טראַנספּאָרט?

You don't have enough money to purchase the merchandise.
ir hot nit genug gelt tsu koyfn di skhoyre.
איר האָט נישט גענוג געלט צו קויפן די סחורה.

How much does the shipping cost and is it in foreign currency?
vi fil kost di shiping aun iz es in fremd krantkayt?
ווי פיל קאָסט די שיפּינג און איז עס אין פרעמד קראַנטקייט?

There is a tax exemption on this income.
es iz do a shtayer bafrayung aoyf dem hakhnose.
עס איז דא אַ שטייַער באַפרייַאונג אויף דעם הכנסה.

My position in the company is marketing and I am responsible for advertising and ads.
mayn shtele in der firme iz farkoyf, aun ikh bin farantvortlekh far gantse reklamen un far reklamieren.
מיין שטעלע אין דער פירמע איז פאַרקויף און איך בין פאַראַנטוואָרטלעך פאַר גאַנצע רעקלאַמען און פאר רעקלאַמירן.

SPORTS - SPORT ספֿאָרט

Basketball - koyshbol קוישבאָל

Soccer - fusbol פֿוסבאָל

Game - shpil שפּיל

Stadium - stadium סטאַדיום

Ball – bol באָל

Player - shpiler שפּילער

To jump - tsu shpringen צו שפּרינגען / **To throw** - tsu varfn צו וואַרפֿן

To kick - tsu brik צו בריק / **To catch** - tsu khapn צו כאַפּן

Coach – einlerner איינלערנער / **Referee** - shoyfet שופֿט

Competition - farmest פֿאַרמעסט

Team - manshaft מאַנשאַפֿט

Teammate – manshaft chaver מאַנשאַפֿט חבר

National team - natsyonaler manshaft נאַציאָנאַלער מאַנשאַפֿט

I like to watch basketball games.
ikh hob lib tsu kukn af koyshbol shpileray.
.איך האָב ליב צו קוקן אויף קוישבאָל שפּילעריַי

Soccer is my favorite sport.
fusbol iz meyn balibste sport.
.פֿוסבאָל איז מיין באַליבסטע ספֿאָרט

To play basketball, you need to be good at throwing and jumping.
tsu shpiln koyshbol, draft ihr gut kenen varfn aun shpringen.
.צו שפּילן קוישבאָל, דאַרפֿט איר גוט קענען וואַרפֿן און שפּרינגען

The national team has a lot of fans.
di natsyanale manshaft hot asakh anhenger.
די נאַציאָנאַלע מאַנשאַפֿט האָט אסאך אַנהענגער

My teammate can't find his helmet.
meyn manshaft ken nisht gefinen zeyn helm.
.מיין מאַנשאַפֿט חבר קען נישט געפֿינען זיין העלם

The coach and the team were on the field during half-time.
der einlerner aun di manshaft zenen geven aoyf dem feld beshas der halb-tseyt.
דער איינלערנער און די מאַנשאַפֿט זענען געווען אויף דעם פֿעלד בשעת דער האַלב-
צייט.

Opponent - kegner קעגנער

Half time - halb tseyt האַלב צייט

Finals – letstns לעצטנס

Scores – cheshbon חשבון

The goal - der tsil דער ציל

A goal - a tsil א ציל

To lose - tsu farlirn צו פֿאַרלירן

A Defeat - a bazign א באַזיגן

To win - tsu gevinen צו געווינען

A victory - a nitsakhun א נצחון

The loser - der farloirener דער פֿאַרלוירענער

The winner - der geviner דער געווינער

Fans – anhenger אנהענגער

Field - feld פעלד

Helmet - helm העלם

Penalty - shtrof שטראָף

Basket - koysh קוייש

The coach needs to bring his team today to meet the new referee.
der koutsh darf brengen zeyn manshaft haynt tsu trefn dem nay shoyfet.

דער איינלערנער דאַרף ברענגען זיין מאַנשאַפֿט היינט צו טרעפֿן דעם ניַעם שופֿט

Our opponents went home after their defeat.
aundzere kegner zaynen aheym geforn nokh zeyer mflh.

אונדזערע קעגנער זיַינען אַהיים געפֿאָרן נאָך זייער מפלה.

I have tickets to a soccer game at the stadium.
ikh hob bileten tsu a fusbol shpil in dem stadyom.

איך האָב בילעטן צו אַ פוסבאָל שפיל אין דעם סטאַדיאַם

The player received a penalty for kicking the ball in the wrong goal.
der shpiler hot bakumen a shtrof far briken di pilke in dem aumrekhtign tsil.

דער שפילער האָט באקומען אַ שטראָף פֿאַר בריקן די פילקע אין דעם אומרעכטיקן ציל.

Not every person likes sports.
nit yeder mentsh hot lieb sportn.

ניט יעדער מענטש האָט ליב ספּאָרטן.

Athlete - Atlet אַטלעט
Olympics – olimpiada אלימפיאדא
World cup prize- velt kos gevins וועלט כּוס געווינס
Bicycle - velosiped וועלאָסיפעד
Cyclist – bitsikleter ביציקלעטער
Swimming - shvimen שווימען
Wrestling - ranglerey ראַנגלעריי
Boxing – boksen באָקסן
Martial arts - marshal kunst מאַרשאל קונסט
Championship – meistershaft מייסטערשאפט
Award - priz פּריז
Tournament - turnamant טאָורנאַמענט
Horseracing - ferd geyug פערד געיאג
Racing – geyug געיאג

Today are the finals for the Olympic Games.
haynt zenen di letzte konkurses far di olimpiad shpieln.
היינט זענען די לעצטע קאָנקורסעס פֿאַר די אָלימפיאד שפילן

Let's see who wins the World Cup.
Lomir zen ver vet gevinen di velt kop.
לאָמיר זען ווער וועט געווינען די וועלט קאָפ.

I want to compete in the cycling championship.
ikh vil konkurirn in di bitsikleter meistershaft.
איך וויל קאָנקורירן אין די ביציקלעטער מייסטערשאפט.

I am an athlete so I must stay in shape.
ikh bin a atlet azoy ikh muzn blaybn in forem.
איך בין אן אטלעט אזוי איך מוז בלייַבן אין פאָרעם.

After my boxing lesson, I want to go and swim in the pool.
nokh meyn baxing lektsye, ikh viln tsu geyn aun shvimen in di bekn.
נאָך מיין באַקסינג לעקציע, איך וויל גיין שווימען אין די שווימבאַסיין.

He will receive an award because he is the winner of the martial-arts tournament.
er vet bakumen a priz vayl er iz der geviner fun di marshal-kunst turnamant.
ער וועט באַקומען אַ פּריז וויַיל ער איז דער געווינער פון די מאַרשאַל-קונסט
טורנאַמאַנט

Exercise – bevegung בעוועגונג
Fitness - toygikayt טויגיקייט
Gym - sportzal ספּאָרטזאַל
Captain - kapitan קאַפּיטאַן / **Judge** - rikhter ריכטער
A match - a konkurs קאָנקורס
Rules - kllim כּללים
Track - shpur שפּור
Trainer - treyner טריינער
Pool (billiards) - bilyards ביליאַרדן
Pool (swimming pool) - shvimbaseyn שווימבאַסיין

The wrestling captain must teach his team the rules of the game.
der ranglerey kapitan muzn lernen zeyn manshaft di kllim fun di shpil.
דער ראַנגלעריי קאַפּיטאַן מוז לערנען זיין מאַנשאַפֿט די כּללים פון די שפּיל.

At the horse-racing competition, the judge couldn't announce the score.
bey di ferd-geyug farmest, der rikhter ken nisht meldn di khezhbn.
ביי די פֿערד גיאַג פֿאַרמעסט, דער ריכטער קען נישט מעלדן די חשבון.

There is a bicycle race at the park today.
es iz a velosiped rase in der park haynt.
עס איז אַ וועלאָסיפּעד גיאַג אין דער פּאַרק היינט.

This fitness program is expensive.
dem toygikeyt program iz tayer.
דעם טויגיקייט פּראָגראַם איז טייַער.

It's healthy to go to the gym every day.
es iz gezunt tsu geyn tsu di sportzal yeder tog.
עס איז געזונט צו גיין צו די ספּאָרטזאַל יעדער טאָג.

Weightlifting is good exercise.
Heiben shvere vog iz gut genitung.
הייבן שווערע וואַג איז גוט געניטונג.

I want to run on the track today.
ikh vil loyfn aoyf der shpur haynt.
איך וויל לויפֿן אויף דער שפּור היינט.

I like to win in billiards.
ikh gleich gevinen in billyards.
איך גלייך געווינען אין ביליאַרדס.

OUTDOOR ACTIVITIES
DROYSNDIKE AKTIVITETN דרויסנדיקע אַקטיוויטעטן

Compass - kompas קאָמפּאַס
Camping - lagern לאַגערן
A camp - a lager אַ לאַגער
Campground – lageren platz לאַגערן פּלאַץ
Tent - getselt געצעלט
Campfire – lager fayer לאַגער פֿײַער
Matches - shvebelekh שוועבעלעך
Lighter – untsinder אָנצינדער
Coal - koyln קוילן
Flame - flam פֿלאַם
The smoke - der roykh דער רויך

There aren't any tents at the campground.
es zenen keyn getseltn in di kampgraund.
עס זענען קיין געצעלטן אין די קאַמפּגראַונד.

I want to sleep in an RV instead of a tent.
ikh vil shlofn in a rv anshtot fun a getselt.
איך וויל שלאָפֿן אין אַ רוו אַנשטאָט פֿון אַ געצעלט.

We can use a lighter to start a campfire.
mir kenen nutsn an untsinder far di lager feier.
מיר קענען נוצן אַן אָנצינדער פֿאַר די לאַגער פֿייער.

We need coal and matches for the trip.
mir darfn koyln aun shvebelekh far di yazde.
מיר דאַרפֿן קוילן און שוועבעלעך פֿאַר די יאַזדע.

Put out the fire because the flames are very high and there is a lot of smoke.
lesh aoys di feyer veyl di flamen zenen zeyer hoykh aun es iz faran asakh roykh.
לעש אויס די פֿייער ווייל די פֿלאַמען זענען זייער הויך און עס איז פֿאַראן אסאך רויך.

There is fog outside and the temperature is below freezing.
es iz do a nepl indroysn aun di temferatur iz nideriker fun frost.
עס איז דא אַ נעפּל אינדרויסן און די טעמפּעראַטור איז נידעריקער פֿון פֿראָסט.

Hike — ekskurziya עקסקורזיע
Hiking trail - ekskurziya shteg עקסקורזיע שטעג
Pocketknife - tashen meser טאשן מעסער
Fishing - fisheray פישעריי
To fish - tsu fish צו פיש
Fishing pole — ventke ווענטקע
Hook - kruk קרוק
A float - a lozn shvimen אַ לאָזן שווימען
A weight - a vog אַ וואָג
Bait - lekekhl לעקעכל
Fishing net - fisheray nets פישעריי נעץ
To hunt - tsu yogen nokh צו יאגן נאך
Rifle - biks ביקס

Where is the fishing store? I need to buy hooks, bait, and a net.
vu iz di fisheray krom? ikh darf koyfn krux, lekekhl aun a nets.
ווו איז די פישעריי קראָם? איך דאַרף קויפן קרוקס, לעקעכל און אַ נעץ.

You can't bring your fishing pole or your hunting rifle to the campground of the State Park because there is a sign there which says, "No fishing and no hunting."
ir kent nisht brengen di ventke oder di geyeg bix tsu di lageren platz fun di shtat park vayl es iz do a shild vos zagt, "keyn fisheray aun keyn geyeg."
איר קענט נישט ברענגען די ווענטקע אָדער די גייעג ביקס צו די לאָגערן פלאָץ פון די שטאַט פּאַרק ווייַל עס איז דאָ אַ שילד וואָס זאָגט, "קיין פישעריי און קיין גייעג."

I enjoy hiking on the trail, with my compass and my pocketknife.
ikh hnah kheyking aoyf der shteg, mit meyn kompas aun meyn keshene.
איך האב הנאה גיין אויף עקסקורזיעס אויפן שטעג, מיט מייַן קאָמפּאַס און מייַן טאַשען מעסער

Don't forget the water bottle in your backpack.
du zalst nisht fargesn di vaser flash in deyn bakpak.
דו זאָלסט נישט פֿאַרגעסן די וואַסער פֿלאָש אין דייַן באַקפּאַק.

ELECTRICAL DEVICES
ELEKTRISHE MAKHSHIRIM עלעקטראָנישע מכשירים

Electronic - elektronik עלעקטראָניק
Electricity - elektre עלעקטרע
Appliance – apparat אפּאראט
Oven - oyvn אויוון
Stove - hrube הרובע
Microwave - meykraveyv מייקראַווייוו
Refrigerator - frijider פרידזשידער
Freezer - frizer פּריזער
Alarm – alarem אלאַרעם
Smoke detector - roykh detektor רויך דעטעקטאָר

He needs to pay his electric bill if he wants electricity.
er darf tsoln zayn elektrishe rekhenung aoyb er vil elektre.
ער דאַרף צאָלן זײַן עלעקטרישע רעכענונג אויב ער וויל עלעקטרע.

I want to purchase a few things at the electronic appliance store.
ikh vil koyfn a por zakhn in di elektronish aparat krom.
איך וויל קויפן אַ פּאָר זאכן אין די עלעקטראָניש אַפּאראט קראָם.

I can't put plastic utensils in the dishwasher.
ikh ken nisht shteln plastik makhsirim in di keylim - vasher.
איך קען נישט שטעלן פּלאַסטיק מכשירים אין די כלים וואַשער

I am going to get rid of my microwave and oven because they are not functioning.
ikh vel avekvarfen meyn meykraveyv aun oyvn vayl zey funksioniren nisht.
איך וועל אוועקוואַרפן מיין מייקראַווייוו און אויוון וויַיל זיי פאַנקסיאָנירן נישט.

The refrigerator and freezer aren't cold enough.
di frijider aun frizer zenen nisht kalt genug.
די פרידזשידער און פּריזער זענען נישט קאַלט גענוג.

Is that annoying sound the alarm clock or the fire alarm?
iz der dulendiker klang fun di alarem zeyger oder di fayer alarem?
איז דער דולענדיקער קלאַנג פון די אלאַרום זייגער אדער די פּייער אלאַרעם

Coffee maker - kave fabrikant קאַווע פאַבריקאַנט
Coffee pot - kave top קאַווע טאָפּ
Toaster - tsubroyner צוברוינער
Dishwasher - keylim vasher כּלים וואַשער.
Laundry machine - vesh mashin וועש מאַשין
Laundry - vesh וועש
Dryer – trikener טריקענער
Fan – ventilator ווענטילאַטור
Air condition - luft tsushtand לופֿט צושטאַנד
Battery - baterie באַטעריִע

The coffee maker and toaster are in the kitchen.
di kave fabrikant aun tsubroyner zenen in der kikh.
די קאַווע פאַבריקאַנט און צוברוינער זענען אין דער קיך.

My washing machine and dryer do not function, therefore I must wash my laundry at the public laundromat.
mayn vashmashin aun triekener ton nit funktsyonirn, deriber ikh muz vashn meyn vesh in di vesherei
מײַן וואַשמאַשין און טריקענער טאָן פונקציאָנירן נישט, דעריבער מוז איך וואַשן מײַן וועש אין די וועשערײַ

Is this fan new?
iz dos ventolator nay?
איז דאָס ווענטאָלאַטאָר נײַ?

Unfortunately, the new air conditioner unit hasn't been delivered yet.
tsum badoyern, di naye luft kandishaner aparat iz nokh nisht ibergegebn.
צום באַדויערן, די נײַע לופֿט אַפּאַראַט איז נאָך נישט איבערגעגעבן.

The smoke detector needs new batteries.
der roykh detektor darf nay bateries.
דער רויך דעטעקטאָר דאַרף נײַ באַטעריעס.

162

Lamp - lomp לאָמפּ
Stereo - steryoufon סטעריאָפאן
A (wall) clock /a watch - a zeyger א זייגער
Vacuum cleaner - vakvm kliner וואַקוום קלינער
Phone - telefon טעלעפאָן
Text message - text onzog טעקסט אָנזאָג
Voice message - shtime onzog שטימע אָנזאָג
Camera - aparat אַפּאַראַט

The clock is hanging on the wall.
der zeyger hengt aoyf der vant.
דער זייגער הענגט אויף דער וואַנט.

The cordless stereo is on the table.
di steryoufon un a shnier iz aoyf dem tish.
די סטעריאָופאן אן אַ שניר איז אויף דעם טיש.

I still have a home telephone.
ikh hob nokh a heym telefon.
איך האָב נאָך אַ היים טעלעפאָן.

I need to buy a lamp and a vacuum cleaner today.
ikh darf heynt koyfn a lomp aun a vakvm kliner.
איך דאַרף היינט קויפן אַ לאָמפ און אַ וואַקוום קלינער.

In the past, cameras were more common. Today, everyone can use their phones to take pictures.
in der fargangenheyt, kameras zenen geven mer geveyntlekh. Haynt, yeder ken nutsn zeyer telefonen tsu nemen bilder.
אין דער פאַרגאַנגענהייט, קאַמעראַס זענעןגעוועןמער געווייינטלעך. היינט, יעדער קענען ניצן זייער טעלעפאאנען צו נעמען בילדער

You can leave me a voice message or send me a text message.
ir kent lozn mir a kul onzog oder shikn mir a text onzog.
איר קענט לאָזן מיר אַ קול אָנזאָג אָדער שיקן מיר אַ טעקסט אָנזאָג.

Flashlight – lamterel לאמטערל
Light - likht ליכט
Furnace - aoyvn אויוון
Heater - baheytsung באַהייצונג
Cord - shnur שנור
Charger - tsharjer טשאַרדזשער
Outlet – kontakt קאָנטאַקט
Doorbell – glekel גלעקל
Lawnmower – groz-shnayder גראָז־שנײַדער

The lights don't function when there is a blackout. Therefore, I must rely on my flashlight.
di leyts ton nit funktsyonirn ven es iz do a farfinsterung. Deriber ikh muz farlozn zikh oif meyn lamterl.
די ליכט פונקציאָנירט נישט ווען עס איז דאַ אַ פאַרפינסטערונג, דעריבער מוז איך פאַרלאָזן זיך אויף מיין לעמטערל

I can't hear the doorbell.
ikh ken nisht hern di glekel.
איך קען נישט הערן די גלעקל

There is a higher risk of causing a house fire from an electric heater than a furnace.
es iz do a hekher einshtel fun farshafn a hoyz fayer fun an elektrishe heitzung vi fun an aoyvn.
עס איז דאַ אַ העכער איינשטעל פון פאַרשאַפן אַ הויז פייער פון אַן עלעקטרישע הייצונג ווי פון אַן אויוון.

I need to connect the cord to the outlet.
ikh darf farbindn di shnur tsu di kontakt
איך דאַרף פאַרבינדן די שנור צו די קאָנטאַקט.

His lawnmower is very noisy.
zeyn gruz shneider macht a goiser tumul.
זיין גראַז שניידער מאַכט אַ גרויסער טומל

164

TOOLS - MAKHSHIRIM מכשירים

Toolbox - makhshirim מכשירים
Carpenter - stolyer סטאָליער
Hammer - hamer האַמער
Saw - zeg זעג
Axe - hak האַק
A drill - a boyer אַ בויער
To drill - tsu boyer צו בויער
Nail - negl נעגל
A screw - a shroyf אַ שרויף
Screwdriver - shroyfn-tsyer שרויפנציער
A wrench - a muter-shlisl אַ מוטער-שליסל
Pliers - tsvang צוואַנג
Paintbrush - molen barsht מאָלן באַרשט
To paint - tsu moln צו מאָלן
The paint - di farb די פֿאַרב

The carpenter needs nails, a hammer, a saw, and a drill.
der stolyer darf negl, a hamer, a zeg aun a boyer.
דער סטאָליער דאַרף נעגל, אַ האַמער, אַ זעג און אַ בויער.

The string is very long. Where are the scissors?
di shtrikl iz zeyer lang. vau zenen di sher?
די שטריקל איז זייער לאַנג. וואו זענען די שער?

The screwdriver is in the toolbox.
di shroyfn - tsyer iz in di mkhshirim.
די שרויפנציער איז אין די מכשירים.

This tool can cut through metal.
der getsayg ken shnaydn durkh metal.
דער געצייַג קען שנייַדן דורך מעטאַל.

The ladder is next to the tools.
der leyter iz lebn di mkhshirim.
דער לייטער איז לעבן די מכשירים.

Ladder - leyter לײטער
Rope - shtrik שטריק / **String -** shtrikl שטריקל
A scale - a vog אַ װאָג
Measuring tape - mestn teyp מעסטן טײפּ
Machine - mashin מאַשין
A lock - a shlos אַ שלאָס
Locked - farshfart פֿאַרשפֿאַרט
To lock - tsu shliessen צו שליסן
Equipment – oisrikht אױסריכט
Metal - Metal מעטאַל
Steel - shtol שטאָל
Iron - ayzn אײַזן
Broom - bezem בעזעם / **Dustpan –** shtoyb sheivele שטױב שײװעלע
Mop – vish beizem װישבעזעם / **Sponge -** shvam שװאָם
Bucket - emer עמער
Shovel - ridl רידל / **A trowel –** kelnia קעלניע

I must buy a brush to paint the walls.
ikh muz koyfn a barsht tsu moln di vent.
איך מוז קױפֿן אַ באַרשט צו מאָלן די װענט.

The paint bucket is empty.
der farb emer iz leydik.
דער פֿאַרב עמער איז לײדיק.

It's better to tie the shovel with a rope in my truck.
es iz beser tsu bindn di ridl mit a shtrik in meyn trok.
עס איז בעסער צו בינדן די רידל מיט אַ שטריק אין מײַן פּיק-אַרױף טראָק.

How can I fix this machine?
vi ken ikh farrikhtn dem mashin?
װי קען איך פֿאַרריכטן דעם מאַשין?

The broom and dustpan are with the rest of my cleaning equipment.
di bezem aun shtoyb pan zenen mit di resht fun meyn reynikung oysrikht.
די בעזעם און שטיב פֿאַן זענען מיט די רעשט פֿון מײַן רײיניקונג װיסריכט.
Where did you put the mop and the bucket?
vu hostu geleygt di vishbeizem aun di emer?
װוּ האסטו געלײיגט די װישבעזעם און די עמער?

CAR - MASHIN מאַשין

Engine - motor מאָטאָר
Ignition – tzindung צינדונג
Automatic - otomatish אטאמאטיש
Manual – hant האנט
Gear shift - gang iberruk גאַנג יבעררוק
Seat – zits זיץ
Seatbelt - zits gartl זיץגאַרטל
Brakes – tormaz טאָרמאז
Hand brake - hant tormoz האַנט טאָרמאָז
Airbag - Airbag אירבאַג

I must take my car to my mechanic because there is a problem with the ignition.
ikh muzn nemen meyn mashin tsu meyn mekhaniker vayl es iz a problem mit di tzindung
איך מוז נעמען מיין מאַשין צו מיין מעכאַניקער ווייל עס איז אַ פּראָבלעם מיט די צינדונג.

What happened to the engine?
vos iz geshen mit di motor?
וואָס איז געשען מיט די מאָטאָר?

The seat is missing a seat belt.
der zitsplats iz felndik a zitsplats gartl.
דער זיצפּלאַץ איז פעלנדיק אַ זיצפּלאַץ גאַרטל.

The brakes are new in this car
di brakes zenen nay in dem mashin
די בראַקעס זענען נייַ אין דעם מאַשין

This car doesn't have a handbreak.
der mashin hut nisht a hant tormoz.
דער מאַשין האָט נישט אַ האַנט טאָרמאָז.

There is an airbag on both the driver side and the passenger side.
es iz do an airbag aoyf di shofer zayt aun di pasazhir zayt.
עס איז דאָ אַן אירבאַג אויף די שאָפער זייַט און די פּאַסאַזשיר זייַט.

My car doesn't have an alarm.
meyn mashin hut nisht kein alarum.
מיין מאַשין האָט נישט קיין אלאַרום

Steering wheel – kerme קערמע
Baby seat – kinder zits קינדער זיץ
Driver seat – firer zits פירער זיץ
Passenger seat - pasazhir zits פּאַסאַזשיר זיץ
Front seat – oiven zits אויוון זיץ
Back seat – inten zits אינטן זיץ
Warning light - varenung likht וואַרענונג ליכט
Button - knepl קנעפּל
Horn (of the car) - horn הֶאָרן
Windshield - vintshoyb ווינטשויב
Windshield wiper - vintshoyb visher ווינטשויב וויישער
Windshield fluid - vintshoyb fliskeit ווינטשויב פֿליסקייט
Rearview mirror – hinterteil shpiegel הינטערטייל שפּיגל
Side mirror - zayt shpigl זײַט שפּיגל
Alarm - alarm אַלאַרם
Window - fentster פֿענצטער

When driving, both hands must be on the steering wheel.
ven dreyving, beyde hent muzn zeyn aoyf di kerme.
.ווען מען פֿאַרט, ביידע הענט מוזן זיין אויף די קערמע

The baby seat is in the back seat.
di kinder zits iz fun unten.
.די קינדער זיץ איז פֿון אונטן

The warning light button is located next to the stirring wheel.
di varenung likht iz lebn di kerme.
די וואַרענונג ליכט איז לעבן די קערמע

The windshield and all four of my car windows are cracked.
der vintshoyb aun ale fir mashin fentster zenen gekrakh.
דער ווינטשויב און אַלע פיר מאַשין פֿענצטער זענען געקראַקט

I want to clean my rear-view mirror and my side mirrors.
ikh viln reiniken meyn hinterteil shpigl aun meyn zayt shpiglen.
איך ווילן רייניקן מיין הינטערטייל שפּיגל און מיין זײַט שפּיגלׁען

Door handle - tir hentel טיר הענטל
Spare tire – rezerv raif רעזערוו רייף
Trunk – bagazhnik באגאזשניק
Hood (of the vehicle) - kapter קאַפּטער
Driver's license – shofir litsentz שאָפיר ליצענץ
License plate - litsentz teler ליצענץ טעלער
Gasoline - gazolin גאַזאָלין
Low fuel - niderik brenvarg נידעריק ברענוואַרג
Flat tire - flakh rayf פלאַך רייַף
Crowbar – shaber שאבער
Wrench – muter shlisel מוטער שליסל

Does this car have a spare tire in the trunk?
Hot dem oyto a rezerve rayf in dem bagazhnik?
האָט דעם אױטאָ אַ רעזערווע רייַף אין דעם באאגאזשניק?

Please, close the car door.
bite farmakh di tir fun oto.
ביטע פארמאַך די טיר פון אױטאָ

Where is the nearest gas station?
vu iz di nonste gaz stantsye?
ווו איז די נאנסטע גאַז סטאַנצסיע?

The windshield wipers are new.
di vintshoyb vishers zenen nay.
די ווינטשויב ווישערס זענען נייַ.

The door handle on the driver's side doesn't function.
di tir hentel aoyf di shofer zayt tut nisht arbetn.
די טיר הענטל אױף די שאָפער זייַט טוט נישט אַרבעטן.

Your license plate has expired.
deyn derloybenish teler iz aoysgegangen.
דיין ליצענץ טעלער איז אױסגעגאאנגען.

I want to renew my driving license today.
ikh vil banayen meyn dreyving derloybenish haynt.
איך וויל באַנייַען מיין שאָפיר ליצענץ הייַנט.

Are the car doors locked?
zenen di mashin tirn farshfart?
זענען די מאַשין טירן פארשפּארט?

NATURE - NATUR אָנטור

A plant - a geviks א געוויקס
Forest - vald וואַלד
Tree - boym בוים
Trunk - shtam שטאַם
Branch - tsvayg צווייַג
Leaf - blat בלאַט
Root - vortsl וואָרצל
Flower - blum בלום
Petal – krohnbletel קרוינבלעטל
Blossom - blyen בליִען
Stem – shtengel שטענגל
Seed - zoymen זוימען

I want to collect a few leaves during the fall.
ikh vil zamlen a bisl bleter beshas di harbst.
איך וויל זאַמלען אַ ביסל בלעטער בשעת די האַרבסט.

There aren't any plants in the desert during this season.
es zenen keyn gevixn in der mdbr in dem sezon.
עס זענען קיין געוויקסן אין דער מדבר אין דעם סעזאָן.

The trees need rain.
di beymer darfn regn.
די ביימער דאַרפֿן רעגן.

The trunk, the branches, and the roots are all parts of the tree.
der shtam, di tsveygn, aun di ruts zenen ale teyln fun dem boym.
דער שטאַם, די צווייַגן, און די וואָרצלען זענען אַלע טיילן פֿון דער בוים

The orchid needs to bloom because I want to see its beautiful petals.
di orkhidee darf blyen vayl ikh vil zen di sheyne kroinbletlekh.
די אָרכידעע דאַרף בליִען ווייַל איך וויל זען די שיינע קרוינבלעטלעך

Where can I plant the seeds?
vi ken ikh einflantzen di zoimen?
ווי קען איך איינפֿלאַנצן די זוימען

170

Rose - royze רויזע

Nectar - nekter נעקטער

Pollen - shtoyb שטויב

Vegetation – vaksunsg וואקסונג

Bush - kust קוסט

Grass - groz גראָז

Rain forest - regn vald רעגן וואַלד

Tropical - tropikal טראָפּיקאַל

Palm tree – palme boim פּאלמע בוים

Season - sezon סעזאָן

Spring - friling פרילינג

Summer - zumer זומער

Winter - vinter ווינטער

Autumn - harbst האַרבסט

My rose bushes are beautiful.

mayn royz tzveigen zenen sheyn.

מײַנע רויזן צוווײַגן זענען שײַן.

I must trim the grass and vegetation in my garden.

ikh muz shnayden di groz aun vaksung in meyn gortn.

איך מוז שנײַדן די גראָז און וואקסונג אין מיין גאָרטן.

The rain forest is a nature preserve.

der regn vald iz a natur rezerv.

דער רעגן וואַלד איז אַ נאַטור רעזערווע.

Palm trees can only grow in a tropical climate.

palme beymer kenen vaxn bloyz in a trapishe klimat.

פּאלמע בײַמער קענען וואקסן בלויז אין אַ טראָפּישע קלימאַט.

I am allergic to pollen.

ikh bin alerjik tsu shtoyb.

איך בין אַלערדזשיק צו שטויב.

Is the nectar from the flower sweet?

iz der nekter fun di blum zis?

איז דער נעקטער פון די בלום זיס?

Be careful because the plant stem can break very easily.

Zeyt opgehit vayl di fabrik stem kenen tzubrekhn zeyer leykht.

זייט פּאַרזיכטיק ווײַל די געוויקס שטעענגל קענען צוברעכן זייער לייכט

Ocean - akean אקעאן
Waterfall - vaserfal וואסערפאל
Lake - taykh טײַך
River - teykh טײך
Sea - yam ים
Canal - kanal קאנאל
Swamp - zump זומפ
Mountain - barg באַרג
Hill - bergl בערגל
Rainbow - regnboygn רעגנבויגן
Cloud - volkn וואָלקן
Lightning - blits בליץ
Thunder - duner דונער
Rain - regn רעגן
Sky - himl הימל

There is a rainbow above the waterfall.
Aoybn fun di vaserfal iz a regnboygn.
אויבן פון די וואַסערפאַל איז אַ רעגנבויגן.

The ocean is bigger than the sea.
der okean iz greser vi der yam.
דער אָקעאַן איז גרעסער ווי דער ים.

From the mountain, I can see the river.
fun barg, ikh ken zen dem taykh.
פֿון באַרג, איך קען זען דעם טײַך.

There aren't any clouds in the sky.
es zenen nisht do keyn valkns in der himl.
עס זענען נישט דא קיין וואלקנס אין דער הימל.

I see the lightning from my window.
ikh ze di blitsn fun meyn fentster.
איך זע די בליצן פון מיין פענצטער.

I can hear the thunder from outside.
ikh her dem duner fun droysen.
איך הער דעם דונער פון דרויסען.

172

Snow - shney שניי
Ice - eyz אייז
Hail - hogl האָגל
Fog - nepl נעפל
Wind - vint ווינט
Air - luft לופט
Dew - toy טוי
Sunset - zun untergang זון אונטערגאַנג
Sunrise – zun oifgang זון אויפגאַנג
Deep - tif טיף
Shallow - plitke פליטקע

I want to see the sunset from the hill.
ikh vil zen di zun untergang fun dem bergl.
איך וויל זען די זון אונטערגאַנג פון דעם בערגל.

The lake has a shallow part and a deep part.
der teich hat a plitke teyl aun a tifer teyl.
דער טייך האַט אַ פליטקע טייל און אַ טיפער טייל.

I don't like the wind.
ikh hob nisht lib vint.
איך האָב נישט ליב דער ווינט.

The air on the mountain is very clear.
di luft aoyfn barg iz zeyer klar.
די לופט אויפן בארג איז זייער קלאר.

Every dawn, there is dew on the leaves of my plants.
yeder fartog, es iz toy aoyf di bleter fun meyn gevixn.
יעדער פאַרטאָג, עס איז טוי אויף די בלעטער פון מיין געוויקסן.

Is this ice or hail?
iz dos eyz oder hogl?
איז דאָס אייז אָדער האָגל?

I can see the volcano.
ikh ken zen dem vulkan.
איך קען זען דעם וווּלקאַן.

Today we hope to see snow.
heynt hafn mir tsu zen shney.
היינט האפן מיר צו זען שניי.

World - velt וועלט
Earth - erd ערד
Sun - zun זון
Moon - lbnh לבנה
Full moon - gants lbnh גאַנץ לבנה
Star - shtern שטערן
Planet – planet פּלאַנעט
Fire - fayer פֿײַער
Heat - hits היץ
Humidity – feikhtkeit פֿײַכטקײַט
Island - inzl אינזל
Cave - heyl הייל
Agriculture - agrikultur אַגריקולטור

The moon and the stars are beautiful in the night sky.
di lbnh aun di shtern zenen sheyn in di nakht himl.
די לבנה און די שטערן זענען שיין אין די נאַכט הימל.

The earth is a planet.
di erd iz a planet.
די ערד איז אַ פּלאַנעט.

The heat today is unbearable.
di hits heynt iz aumdertreglekh.
די היץ היינט איז אומדערטרעגלעך.

At the beach there is fresh air.
aoyf dem breg es iz frish luft.
אויף דעם ברעג עס איז פריש לופט.

I want to sail to the island to see the sunrise.
ikh vil zeglen tsu der inzl tsu zen di zun ufgang.
איך וויל זעגלען צו דער אינזל צו זען די זונאויפגאַנג.

We live in a beautiful world.
mir lebn in a sheyn velt.
מיר לעבן אין אַ שיין וועלט.

Public park - folkspark פֿאלקספֿארק
National park - natsyonaler park נאַציאָנאַלער פֿאַרק
Rock - shteyn שטיין
Stone - shteyn שטיין
Agriculture - agrikultur אַגריקולטור
Ground - erd ערד
Soil - bodn באָדן
Sea shore - im breg ים ברעג
Seashell – yam multerl ים מולטערל
Dawn - fartog פֿאַרטאָג
Ray – shtrol שטראל
Dry - trukn טרוקן
Wet - nas נאַס
Weeds - vildgroz ווילדגראָז
A stick - a shtekn אַ שטעקן
Dust - shtoyb שטויב

Parts of the cave are dry and other parts are wet.
teyln fun di heyl zenen trukn aun andere teyln zenen nas.
טיילן פֿון די הייל זענען טרוקן און אנדערע טיילן זענען נאַס.

There is dust from the fire in the park.
es iz shtoyb fun di fayer in dem park.
עס איז שטויב פֿון די פּייַער אין דעם פֿאַרק.

I want to collect seashells from the seashore.
ikh vil klaybn yam multerlech fun di breg.
איך וויל קלייַבן ים מולטערלעך פֿון די ברעג.

There are too many stones in the soil, so it's impossible to use this area for agricultural purposes.
es zenen du tsu fil shteyner in dem bodn azoy es iz aummeglekh tsu nutsn dem shtkh far landvirtshaftlekh tsvekn.
עס זענען דא צופיל שטיינער אין דעם באָדן אַזוי עס איז אוממעגלעך צו נוצן דעם שטח פֿאַר לאַנדווירטשאַפֿטלעך צוועקן.

Why are there so many weeds growing by the swamp?
farvos zenen du azoy fil vildgroz vos vaxn durkh dem zump?
פֿאַרוואָס זענען דא אַזוי פֿיל ווילדגראַז וואָס וואַקסן דורך דעם זומפֿ?

ANIMAL - KHAYE חיה

Pet – gletling גלעטלינג
Mammals – zoig khaya זויג חיה
Dog - hunt הונט
Cat - kats קאַץ
Parrot - papugay פּאַפּוגײַ
Pigeon - toyb טויב
Pig - khzir חזיר
Sheep - sheps שעפּס
Cow - ku קו
Bull - bul ביק
Donkey - eyzl אײזל
Horse - ferd פערד
Camel - kemel קעמעל

I have a dog and two cats.
ikh hob a hunt aun tsvey kets.
איך האָב אַ הונט און צוויי קעץ.

There is a bird on the tree.
aoyf dem boym iz a foygl.
אויף דעם בוים איז אַ פויגל.

I want to go to the zoo to see the animals.
ikh viln tsu geyn tsu der zoologisher gortn tsu zen di khius.
איך וויל גיין צו דער זאָאָלאָגישער גאָרטן צו זען די חיות.

My daughter wants a pet horse.
meyn tokhter vil a libling ferd.
מיין טאָכטער וויל אַ גלעטלינג פערד.

A pig, a sheep, a donkey, and a cow are considered farm animals.
a khzir, a sheps, an eyzl aun a ku zenen gehaltn vi farm khayos.
אַ חזיר, אַ שעפּס, אַן אייזל און אַ קו זענען געהאַלטן ווי פאַרם חיות

Rodent – nuger נוגער
Mouse - maz מויז
Rat - rats ראַץ
Rabbit - kinigl קיניגל
Hamster - Hamster האַמסטער
Duck - katshke קאַטשקע
Goose - gandz גאַנדז
Turkey - indik אינדיק
Chicken - hindl הינדל
Poultry - of אָף
Squirrel - veverke וועװערקע

I want a hamster as a pet.
ikh vil a hamster vi a shtub khaye.
איך װיל אַ האַמסטער װי אַ שטוב חיה.

A camel is a desert animal.
a keml iz a mdbr khih.
אַ קעמל איז אַ מדבר חיה.

Can I put ducks, geese, and turkeys inside my coop?
ken ikh shteln katshkes, genz aun indigen in meyn katukh?
קען איך שטעלן קאַטשקעס, גענז און אינדיגן אין מיין קאַטוך

We have rabbits and squirrels in our yard.
mir hobn kinigl aun skveralz in aundzer hoyf.
מיר האָבן קיניגלעך און וויעװערקעס אין אונדזער הויף

It's cruel to keep a parrot inside a cage.
es iz groyzam tsu haltn a papugay in a shtayg.
עס איז גרויזאַם צו האַלטן אַ פּאַפּוגייַ אין אַ שטייַג.

There are many pigeons in the city.
es zenen file pijanz in der shtot.
עס זענען פיל טויבן אין דער שטאָט.

Mice and rats are rodents.
meiz aun rats zenen nugers
מייז און ראַצן זענען נוגערס

Lion – leyb לייב
Hyena - hyene היענע
Leopard - lempert לעמפּערט
Panther - panter פּאַנטער
Elephant - helfand העלפֿאַנד
Rhinoceros – nozhorn נאזהאָרן
Hippopotamus – hipopotam היפּאָפּאָטאַם

There are a lot of animals in the forest.
es zenen du asakh khayos in dem vald.
עס זענען דא אַסאך חיות אין דעם וואַלד.

The most dangerous animal in Africa is not the lion, it's the hippopotamus.
di merstn geferlekh khaye in afrike iz nisht der leyb, es iz di khipapatam.
די מערסטן געפֿערלעך חיה אין אפֿריקע איז נישט דער לייב, עס איז די היפּאָפּאַטאַם

It's usually very difficult to see a leopard in the wild.
es iz gevendlich zeyer shver tsu zen a lempert in di vildenish.
עס איז געוועגדליך זייער שווער צו זען אַ לעמפּערט אין די ווילדעניש.

Elephants and rhinoceroses are known as very aggressive animals.
helfandn aun nozhornen zenen bakant vi zeyer aggressive khayos.
העלאַפֿאַנדן און נאזהאַרנען זענען באקאַנט ווי זייער אַגרעסיוו חיות.

I saw a hyena and a panther at the safari yesterday.
ikh hob nekhtn gezen a hyene aun a panter aoyf der safari.
איך האָב נעכטן געזען אַ היענע און אַ פּאַנטער אויף דער סאַפֿאַרי.

Fox - fux פוקס
Wolf - valf וואלף
Weasel - vizel וויזעל
Bear - ber בער
Tiger - tiger טיגער
Deer - hirsh הירש
Monkey - malpe מאַלפּע
Otter - oter אָטער
Bat - fledermoyz פלעדערמויז

A wolf is much bigger than a fox.
a volf iz fil greser vi a fux.
א וואָלף איז פיל גרעסער ווי אַ פוקס.

Are there bears in this forest?
zenen faran bern in dem vald?
זענען פאראן בערן אין דעם וואלד?

Bats are the only mammals that can fly.
fledermoyzn zenen di eynsike zoigers vos kenen flyen.
פלעדערמויזן זענען די איינסיקע זויגערס וואָס קענען פליען.

The largest member of the cat family is the tiger.
der grester mitglid fun der kats mshpkhh iz der tiger.
דער גרעסטער מיטגליד פון דער קאַץ משפחה איז דער טיגער.

Deer hunting is forbidden in the national park.
hirsh geyeg iz farbotn in di natzionaln park.
הירש גייעג איז פארבאָטן אין די נאַציאנאלן פאַרק.

There are many monkeys on the branches of the trees.
es zenen do a sakh malpes aoyf di tsveygn fun di beymer.
עס זענען דאָ אַסאַך מאַלפּעס אויף די צווייגן פון די ביימער.

Bird - foygl פֿויגל
Crow - krou קראָו
Stork – bushl בושל
Vulture – grif גריף
Eagle - odler אָדלער
Owl – sove סאָווע
Peacock - pave פּאַווע
Reptile – reptilye רעפּטיליע
Turtle - tsherepakhe טשערעפּאַכע
Snake - shlang שלאַנג
Lizard - yashtsherke יאַשטשערקע
Crocodile - krokodil קראָקאָדיל
Frog - zhabe זשאַבע

An eagle and an owl are birds of prey, however vultures are scavengers.
An udler un a sova zenen roibfoigel, ober di vultchers zenen skavandzheren.
אַן אָדלער און אַ סאָווע זענען רויב פֿייגל, אָבער וואַלטשערז זענען סקאַוואַנדזשערן.

Crows are very smart.
krouz zenen zeyer klug.
קראָוז זענען זייער קלוג.

I want to see the stork migration in Europe.
ikh vil zen di bushl migratziye in eyrope.
איך וויל זען די בושל מיגראַציע אין אייראָפּע.

Don't buy a fur coat!
koyft nisht keyn futer!
קויפֿט נישט קיין פֿוטער!

Butterflies and peacocks are colorful.
flaterlekh aun pavkes zenen farbik.
פֿלאַטערלעך און פּאַווקעס זענען פֿאַרביק

Some snakes are poisonous.
etlekhe shlangen zenen samik.
עטלעכע שלאַנגען זענען סאַמיק.

Seal – yam hunt ים הונט
Whale - valfish וואַלפיש
Dolphin - delfin דעלפין
Fish - fish פיש
Shark - hayfish הייַפיש
Wing - fligl פֿליגל
Feather - feder פֿעדער
Tail - ek עק
Fur - futer פֿוטער
Scales - shupn שופּן
Fins – flusfeder פֿלוספֿעדער
Horns - herner הערנער
Claws - kreln קרעלן

Is that the sound of a cricket or a frog?
iz dos der klang fun a tchirkun oder a zhabe?
?איז דאָס דער קלאַנג פֿון אַ טשירקון אָדער אַ זשאַבע

Lizards, crocodiles, and turtles belong to the reptile family.
Yashtsherkes, krokodiln, tcherepakhes, gehern tsu di reptilye mishpokheh.
יאַשטשערקעס, קראָקאָדילן און טשערעפּאַכעס געהערן צו די רעפּטיליע משפּחה

I want to see the fish in the lake.
ikh vil zen di fish in der ozere.
.איך וויל זען די פֿיש אין דער אָזערע

There were a lot of seals basking at the ocean last week.
letste vokh hobn zikh asakh yam hunt gevaremt zich biem yam.
לעצטע וואָך האָבן זיך אַסאַך ים הינט געוואַרעמט זיך ביים ים

A whale is not a fish.
a valfish iz nisht keyn fish.
.אַ וואַלפיש איז נישט קיין פֿיש

Conversational Yiddish Quick and Easy

Insect - insekt אינסעקט
A cricket - a gril גריל
Ant - murashke מוראשקע
Termite - termit טערמיט
A fly - a flig א פליג
Butterfly - flaterl פלאַטערל
Worm - vorem וואָרעם
Mosquito – moskit מאסקיט
Flea - floy פלוי
Lice – layz לייז
A roach - zhuk זשוק
Bee - bin בין

I want to buy mosquito spray.
ikh vil koyfn moskit shprits.
איך וויל קויפן מאסקיט שפּריץ.

I need antiseptic for my bug bites.
ikh darf antiseptik far meyn zhuk bites.
איך דאַרף אַנטיסעפּטיק פֿאַר מיין זשוק ביסן.

I hope there aren't any worms, ants, or flies in the bag of sugar.
ikh hof az es zenen nisht do keyn verem, murashkes oder fligen in di
zekl fun tsuker.
איך האָפֿ אַז עס זענען נישט דא קיין ווערעם, מוראשקעס אָדער פליגן אין די זעקל
פון צוקער.

Bees are very important for the environment.
binen zenen zeyer vikhtik far di svive.
בינען זענען זייער וויכטיק פֿאַר די סוויווע.

Beetles are my favorite insects.
Di djuken zenen meyn balibste insektn.
די דזשוקען זענען מיין באַליבסטע אינסעקטן.

I need to call the exterminator because there are fleas, roaches, and termites in my house.
ikh darf rufn dem exterminator vayl es zenen do floyn, zhukn aun
termiten in meyn hoyz.
איך דאַרף רופן דעם עקסטערמינאַטאָר ווייַל עס זענען פלויען, זשוקן און טערמיטעס
אין מיין הויז.

182

Spider – shpeen שפּין
Scorpion - skorpyon סקאָרפּיאָן
Snail - shnek שנעק
Invertebrates – onshederedik אָנשדרההדיק
Shrimps - shrimp שרימפּ
Clams - klamz קלאָמז
Crab - krab קראַב
Octopus - sprut ספּרוט
Starfish - starfish סטאַרפיש
Jellyfish - jellifish דזשעלליפיש

An octopus has eight tentacles.
a sprut hat akht taperlekh
א ספּרוט האט אַכט טאַפּערלעך

A jellyfish is a common dish in Asian culture.
a jellifish iz a proste essen in asyan kultur.
א. דזשעלליפיש איז אַ פּראָסט עסן אין אַסיאַן קולטור

The museum has a large collection of invertebrate fossils.
der muzey hat a groys zamlung fun invertabreyt fasiln
דער מוזיי האט אַ גרויס זאַמלונג פון אָנשדרההדיק פאַסילן.

I have crabs and starfish in my aquarium.
ikh hob krabs aun starfish in meyn akvarium.
איך האָב קראַבס און סטאַרפיש אין מיין אַקוואַריום.

Certain types of spiders and scorpions can be dangerous.
Etlikhe tipen fun shpinen aun skorpyanen kenen zeyn geferlekh.
עטליכע טיפּן פון שפּינען און סקאָרפּיאַנען קענען זיין געפערלעך.

Is there a snail inside the shell?
iz es a shnek in di shol?
איז עס אַ שנעק אין די שאָל?

RELIGION, CELEBRATIONS, & CUSTOMS
RELIGYE, FEIERUNGEN, & MINHAGIM
מינהגים & ,פייערונגען ,רעליגיע

God - got גָאט

Bible - bibl ביבל

Adam - adm אדם / **Eve** - khuh חוה

Garden of Eden / heaven - gn edn גן עדן

Angels - mlakhim מלאכים

Priest (in Judaism) - khohn כהן

Prayer - sfilh תפילה

Blessing - brkhh ברכה / **To bless** - tsu bentshn צו בענטשן

Religion - religye רעליגיע

What is your religion?
vas iz deyn religye?
?וואס איז דיין רעליגיע

Many religions use the bible.
a sakh religyons nutsn di bibl.
אַ סך רעליגיעס נוצן די ביבל.

We have faith in miracles.
mir hobn amunh in nesem.
מיר האָבן אמונה אין נסים.

Adam and Eve were the first humans and they lived in the Garden of Eden.
adom aun chava zenen geven di ershte mentshn, aun zey hoben gelebt in gan eden.
אדם און חוה זענען געוואען די ערשטע מענטשן און זיי האבן געלעבט אין גן עדן.

When do I need to say the blessing?
ven darf ikh zagn di brkhh?
?וועז דארף איך זאגן די ברכה

I must say a prayer for the holiday.
ikh muz zagn a sflh farn ium tub.
איך מוז זאגן א תפלה פארן יום טוב.

The angels came from heaven.
di mlakhim zenen gekumen fun gn edn.
די מלאכים זענען געקומען פון הימל.

184

Holy - heylik הייליק
Faith - amunh אמונה
Miracle - ns נס
Prophet - nbya נביא
Moses - mshh משה
Messiah - mshikh משיח
Noah - nkh נח / **Ark** - arun ארון
Ten commandments -aseres hadibros עשרת הדברות
To pray - tsu davnen צו דאוונען
Genesis - brashis בראשית
Exodus – shemos שמות / **Leviticus** - vayikra ויקרא
Numbers - bamidbar במדבר / **Deuteronomy** - devorim דברים
The five books of Moses - chamushei chumshei torah חמושי חומשי תורה

Aaron, the brother of Moses, was the first priest.
ahrn, der bruder fun mshh, iz geven der ershter khhn.
אהרן, דער ברודער פון משה, איז געווען דער ערשטער כהן.

The story of Noah's Ark and the flood is very interesting.
di geshikhte fun noakh's teiva aun di mbul iz zeyer interesant.
די געשיכטע פון נח'ס תיבה און די מבול איז זייער אינטערעסאנט.

Moses had to climb up on Mount Sinai to receive the Ten Commandments from God.
mshh hot gemuzt aroyfkrikhn aoyfn barg sini tsu bakumen fun got di eshrs hdbrus.
משה האָט געמוזט אַרויפֿקריכן אויפֿן באַרג סיני צו באַקומען פֿון גאָט די עשרת הדברות.

The Five Books of the Moses are Genesis, Exodus, Leviticus, Numbers, and Deuteronomy.
di chamushei shumshei torah zenen berashis, shemos, vayikra, bameedbar aun devorim..
די חמושי חומשי תורה פון משה זענען בראשית,שמות, ויקרא, במדבר און דברים

Moses was considered as the prophet of all prophets.
mshh iz geven batrakht vi der nbya fun ale nbyaim.
משה איז געווען באטראכט ווי דער נביא פון אלע נביאים.

My favorite book of the bible is the Book of Prophets.
mayn balibste bukh fun di bibl iz der sfr fun nbyaim.
מײַן באַליבסטע בוך פֿון די ביבל איז דער ספר פֿון נביאים.

Jew - yid ייד / **Judaism** - yidishkeyt יידישקייט
Religious – frum פרום
Synagogue - bis hkhnss בית הכנסת
Kosher - khshr כשר

I want to keep kosher.
ikh vil haltn khshrus
איך וויל האלטן כשר.

The Jews worship at the synagogue.
di yidn davenenin der shul.
די יידן דאוועננען אין דער שול.

The Tanakh is a holy book which tells the story of the Jewish nation and includes many miracles.
di tanakh iz a heylike bukh vos dertseylt di geshikhte fun di eydishe folk aun iz Kollel asakh nisim.
די תּנ״ך איז אַ הייליקע בוך וואָס דערצ יילט די געשיכטע פון די יידישע פאָלק און איז כולל אסאך נסים

The three forefathers are Abraham, Isaac, and Jacob.
di drey abus zenen abrhm, itskhk aun yekb.
די דריי אבות זענען אברהם, יצחק און יעקב.

The Torah is divided into 54 portions according to the 54 weeks to be read in the synagogue.
di toyre iz tseteylt in 54 porshanz loyt di 54 vokhn tsu leyenen in di shul.
די תּורה איז צעטיילט אין 54 פּאָרציעס לויט די 54 וואָכן צו לייענען אין די שול.

Saturday, Monday, and Thursday we read the Torah portion of the week.
shbs, mantik aun danershtag leyenen mir di toyre khlk fun der vokh.
שבת, מאָנטיק און דאָנערשטאָג לייענען מיר די תורה חלק פון דער וואָך.

In Judaism, they pray three times a day. Morning prayer, afternoon prayer, and evening prayer.
in eydishkeyt davenen zey drey mal a tag. morgn tefilh, nokhmitog tefilh, aun ovnt tefilh.
אין יידישקייט דאוועננען זיי דריי מאָל אַ טאָג. מאַרגן תפילה, נאָכמיטאָג תפילה, און אָוונט תפילה.

Passover - pskh פּסח
Goblet - bekher בעכער / **Wine** - vayn וויַין
Holidays – yom tov יום טובֿ / **Traditions** - traditsyes טראַדיציעס
Circumcision - bris milh ברית מילה

Where is the goblet of wine for Rosh Hashana?
vau iz der bekher veyn far rash hshnh?
?וואו איז דער בעכער וויַין פאר ראש השנה

I want to fast this year on Yom Kippur.
ikh vil das yar fastn ium khifur.
איך וויל דאס יאר פאסטן יום כּיפּור.

I have a menorah and a dreidel for Hannukah.
ikh hab a mnurh aun a dreydl far khnukhh.
איך האב א מנורה און א דריידל פאר חנוכה.

Passover is my favorite holiday.
pskh iz meyn balibste ium tub.
פּסח איז מיַין באַליבסטע יום טובֿ.

We welcome the Sabbath by lighting candles.
mir bagrisn dem shbs durkh ontsindn likht.
מיר באַגריסן דעם שבת דורך אָנצינדן ליכט.

Where is your yarmulke?
vau iz deyn yarmulke?
?וואו איז דיַין יאַרמולקע

The circumcision is performed on the 8th day after the birth of the child.
di bris milh iz getan aoyf di 8 tog nokh der geburt fun dem kind.
די ברית מילה איז געטאן אויף די 8 טאָג נאָך דער געבורט פון דעם קינד.

There is a large religious Jewish community in this neighborhood.
in dem gegnt iz faran a groyse religyeze idishe khilh.
אין דעם געגנט איז פאראן א גרויסע רעליגיעזע אידישע קהילה.

To learn about the Holocaust and the concentration camps is very important.
tsu lernen vegn dem khurbn aun di kontsentratsye lagern iz zeyer vikhtik.
צו לערנען וועגן דעם חורבן און די קאָנצענטראַציע לאַגערן איז זייער וויכטיק.

Customs - mnhgim מנהגים
Monotheism - monoteizm מאָנאָטעיזם
Old Testament - alte testament אַלטע טעסטאַמענט
New Testament - niu testamen ניו טעסטאַמענט
The Christian Religion - di kristlekhe religye די קריסטלעכע רעליגיע
Church – kirkhe קירכע
Cathedral - katedral קאַטעדראַל
Catholic - katholik קאַטהאָליק
Christian - kristlekh קריסטלעך / **Christianity** - kristntum קריסטנטום
Catholicism - katholisism קאַטהאָליסיסם
Monastery - monasterie מאָנאַסטעריע
Jesus - yoshke יאָשקע / **A cross** - a kreytz קרייץ
Priest (in Christianity) - galekh גאַלעך
Saint – seint סיינט
Holy - heylik הייליק
Holy water - heylik vaser הייליק וואַסער
New Year - niu yor ניו יאר
To sin - tsu zindign צו זינדן
A sin - a zind אַ זינד

The church is open today.
di kirkh iz ofn haynt.
די קירך איז אָפן היינט.

The priest read a psalm from the Bible in front of the congregation.
der galekh hat geleyent farn eulm a lied fun dem bibl.
דער גלח האט געלייענט פֿארן עולם אַ ליד פון דעם ביבל.

I went to pray in the cathedral.
ikh bin gegangen molyen zich in der katedral.
איך בין געגאַנגען מאַליען זיך אין דער קאַטעדראַל.

Happy New Year to all my friends and family.
A git yor tsu ale meyne freynd aun mishpokhe.
אַ גיט יאָר צו אַלע מיין פריינד און משפחה.

Many schools refuse to teach evolution.
file shuln opzogn tsu lernen evolutsye.
פיל שולן אָפזאָגן צו לערנען עוואָלוציע.

Christmas - nitl ניטל
Christmas eve - nitl nakht ניטל נאכט
Christmas tree - nitl boym ניטל בוים
Easter – paskhe פּאסכע
Nuns - monashke מאָנאַשקע
Chapel - kapel קאפּעל
Islam - Islam איסלאם / **Muslim** - Muslim מוסלים
Mohammed - Mohamed מאָהאַממעד / **Mosque –** metshet מעטשעט
Hindu - hindu הינדו / **Buddhist** - buddhist בודהיסט
Temple – tempel טעמפּל

Christians love to celebrate Christmas.
kristn hobn lib tsu fayern nitl.
קריסטן האָבן ליב צו פּיַיערן ניטל.

Is it possible to turn on the lights on my Christmas tree for Christmas Eve?
iz es meglekh ontsutzinden di likht aoyf meyn nitl boym far nitl nakht?
איז עס מעגלעך אָנצוצינדן די ליכט אויף מיַין ניטל בוים פֿאַר ניטל נאכט?

Two more weeks until Easter.
nokh tsvey vokhn biz ister.
נאָך צוויי וואָכן ביז יסטער.

The nuns live in the monastery.
di monashkes lebn in di manasterie.
די מאאנאשקעס לעבן אין די מאַנאַסטעריע

The devil and the demons are from hell.
der shtn aun di beyze geyster zenen fun gihnum.
דער שטן און די שדים זענען פֿון גיהנום.

The Muslims pray at the mosque.
di muslims davnen in di moskve.
די מוסלימען מוליען זיך אין די מעטשעט

In Islam they pray five times a day.
in islam zey davnen finf mal a tog.
אין איסלאם זיי מוליען זיך פֿינף מאל אַ טאג

Both the Hindu and Buddhist religion practice yoga.
Beide hindu aun buddhist religyes firn yoga.
ביידע הינדו און בודהיסט רעליגיעס פֿירן יאָגאַ.

WEDDING AND RELATIONSHIP
KHSUNH AUN BATSIUNG חתונה און באַציִונג

Wedding - khasunah חתונה
Wedding hall - khasunah zal חתונה זאַל
Married - khasunah gehat חתונה געהאט
Civil wedding - tsiviler khasunah ציווילער חתונה
Bride - kalah כלה
Groom - khosn חתן
Ceremony - tseremonye צערעמאָניע
Reception hall - optrog zal אָפּטראָג זאַל
Chapel – kapel קאפעל
Engagement - bashtelung באַשטעלונג
Engagement ring – kalah ring כלה רינג
Wedding ring - khasunah ring חתונה רינג

When is the wedding?
ven iz di khasunah?
?וועו איז די חתונה

We are having the service in the chapel and the reception in the wedding hall.
mir veln hobn di tseremonye in di kapel aun di kabolas ponim in di khasunah zal.
מיר וועלן האָבן די צערעמאָניע אין די קאַפּעל און די קבלת פנים אין די חתונה זאַל.

Three civil weddings are taking place at the courthouse today.
dray tsivile khsunus kumen haynt for in gerikht.
דרײַ ציווילע חתונות קומען הײַנט פֿאַר אין געריכט.

The bride and groom received many presents.
di khsn aun khlh habn bakumen asakh msnus.
די חתן און כלה האבן באקומען אסאך מתנות.

This is my engagement ring and this is my wedding ring.
dos iz meyn bashtelung ring aun dos iz meyn khsunh ring.
דאָס איז מיין כלה רינג און דאָס איז מיין חתונה רינג.

They are finally married, so now it's time for the honeymoon.
zey zenen lesof man un verib, azoy iz itzt di tseyt far di kishvokh
זיי זענען לסוף מאן און וויב, אַזוי איז איצט די צייט פֿאַר די קישוואך

Anniversary - yortog יאָרטאָג
Honeymoon – kishvokh קישוואָך
Fiancé - khosn חתן
Valentine day - valentine tog וואַלענטינע טאָג
Love - libshaft ליבשאַפֿט
To love - tsu libhobn צו ליבהאָבן
In love – farlibt mit פֿאַרליבט מיט

I am in love with her.
ikh bin farlibt mit ir.
איך בין פֿאַרליבט אין איר.

I love her.
ikh hab ir lib.
איך האב איר ליב.

I love him.
ikh hab im lib.
איך האב אים ליב.

I love you.
ikh hab dir lib.
איך האב דיר ליב.

Our anniversary is on Valentine's Day.
aundzer yortog iz aoyf valentines tog.
אונדזער יאָרטאָג איז אויף וואַלענטינעס טאָג.

He decided to propose to his girlfriend. She said "yes" and now they are engaged.
er hut bashlosen tsu forleigen khasene tsu hoben tsu zein khaverte, zi hat gezagt "ya" aun itst zenen zey khosen kalah.
ער האט באַשלאָסן צו פֿאַרלייגן חתונה צו האבן צו זיין חבר'תה. זי האט געזאגט
"יא" און איצט זענען זיי חתן כלה

He is my fiancé now. Next year he will be my husband.
er iz itst meyn khosn. kumedike yor vet er zeyn meyn man.
ער איז איצט מיין חתן, קומעדיקע יאָר וועט ער זיין מיין מאן

Boyfriend - boyfrend בויפרענד
Girlfriend - khaverte כאווערטע
To hug - arumnemen אַרומנעמען
To kiss - tsu kushn צו קושן
A kiss - a kush א קוש
Single - eyn איין
Divorced - geget געגעט
Widow - almnh אלמנה
Romantic - romantish ראָמאַנטיש
Darling - ziskayt זיסקייט
A date – a ranke אַ ראַנקע
A relationship - a sheykhus א שייכות
Husband - man מאַן
Wife - froy פרוי

You are very romantic.
ir zent zeyer romantish.
.איר זענט זייער ראָמאַנטיש

They have a very good relationship.
zey hobn a zeyer gut sheykhus.
.זיי האָבן אַ זייער גוטע שייכות

I am single because I divorced my wife.
ikh bin eyner alein vayl ikh divorsthob geget meyn froy.
.איך בין איינער אליין ווייל איך האב געגעט מיין פרוי

She is my darling and my love.
zi iz meyn libling aun meyn lib.
.זי איז מיין ליבלינג און מיין ליב

I want to kiss you and hug you in this picture.
ikh vil dir kushn aun dir arumnemen in dem bild.
.איך וויל דיר קושן און דיר אַרומנעמען אין דעם בילד

The husband and wife are happily married.
di man aun froy zenen gliklekh baheft.
די מאַן און פרוי זענען גליקלעך פערהייראַט

POLITICS - FALITIK פאָליטיק

Flag - fon פאָן
National anthem - natsyonaler himen נאַציאָנאַלער הימען
Nation - folk פאָלק
National - natsyonal נאַציאָנאל
International - internatsyonaler אינטערנאַציאָנאַלער
Patriot - patryot פאַטריאָט
Symbol - simbol סימבאָל
Peace - sholom שלום
Treaty – opmakh אפמאך
Sanctions - sanktsyes סאַנקציעס

He is a patriot of the nation.
er iz a patryot fun dem folk.
.ער איז אַ פאַטריאָט פון דעם פאָלק

Most countries have a national anthem.
ruv lender hobn a natsyonaler himen.
.רובֿ לענדער האָבן אַ נאַציאָנאַלער הימען

This is a political movement which is supported by the majority.
dos iz a politishe bavegung vos iz geshtitst durkh di merhayt.
.דאָס איז אַ פאָליטישע באַוועגונג וואָס איז געשטיצט דורך די מערהייַט

This flag is the national symbol of the country.
der fon iz di natsyanale simbol fun der mdinh.
.דער פאָן איז די נאַציאנאלע סימבאָל פון דער מדינה

This is all politics.
dos iz alts politik.
.דאָס איז אַלץ פאָליטיק

They must impose sanctions against that country.
zey muzn onton sangshanz kegn dem land.
.זיי מוזן אָנטאָן סאַנגשאַנז קעגן דעם לאַנד

State - shtat שטאַט
Country - land לאַנד
County – kreiz קרייז
Century - yorhundert יאָרהונדערט
Majority - merhayt מערהײט
Local - lakale לאָקאַלע
Campaign - kamfanye קאמפּאַניע
Ambassador - ambasador אַמבאַסאַדאָר
Embassy - ambasade אַמבאַסאַדע
Consulate - konsulat קאָנסולאַט

This is a political campaign to demand independence.
dos iz a politisher kamfanye tsu fodern zelbstshtendikeyt.
דאָס איז אַ פּאָליטישער קאָמפּאַניע צו פאָדערן זעלבסטשטענדיקייט.

There is a difference between state law and local law.
es iz a khiluk tsvishn shtat gezets aun hige gezets.
עס איז אַ חילוק צווישן שטאַט געזעץ און היגע געזעץ.

The ambassador's residence is located near the embassy.
der ambasadors voynort iz lebn der ambasade.
דער אַמבאַסאַדאָרס ווינאָרט איז לעבן דער אַמבאַסאַדע.

I need the phone number and address of the consulate.
ikh darf di telefon numer aun adres fun di konsulat.
איך דארף די טעלעפאָן נומער און אַדרעס פון די קאָנסולאַט.

Are consular services available today?
zenen konsular badinungs bnimtsa haynt?
זענען קאָנסולאַר באַדינונגס בנימצא היינט?

Legal - Legal לעגאל
Law - gezets געזעץ
Illegal - umlegal אומלעגאל
International law - internatsyanale gezets אינטערנאציאנאלע געזעץ
Human rights - mentshnrekht מענטשנרעכט
Punishment - shtrof שטראָף
Torture - paynikung פּײַניקונג
Execution (to kill) – exekutzia עקזעקוציע
Spy - shpyon שפּיאָן
Amnesty - amnistye אַמניסטיע
Political asylum - politishe asil פּאָליטישע אַסיל
Republic - refublik רעפּובליק
Election - valn וואַלן
Candidate - kandidat קאַנדידאַט

There were many protests and riots today.
es zenen geven file protestn aun umruen haynt.
עס זענען געווען פיל פּראָטעסטן און אומרועןhaynt היינט.

The civilian population wanted a revolution.
di tsivile bafelkerung hat gevolt a revalutsye.
די ציווילע באפעלקערונג האט געוואלט א רעוואלוציע.

The politicians want to ask the president to give the captured spy amnesty.
di falitiker viln betn dem frezident er zal gebn dem gekhaftn shfyan amnstye.
די פּאָליטיקער ווילן בעטן דעם פּרעזידענט ער זאל געבן דעם געכאפטן שפּיאן אמנסטיע.

In which county is this legal?
in velkhe kaunti iz das legal?
אין וועלכע קרייז איז דאס לעגאל?

I want to go to the election polls to vote for the new candidate.
ikh vil geyn tsu di valn shtimen farn neyem kandidat.
איך וויל גיין צו די וואַלן שטימען פארן נייעם קאַנדידאַט.

Dictator - diktator דיקטאַטאָר
Citizen - birger בירגער
Resident - eynvaoyner איינוואוינער
Immigrant - imigrant אימיגראנט
Public - tsibur ציבור
Private - Privat פּריוואַט
Government - regirung רעגירונג
Revolution - revolutsye רעוואָלוציע
Civilian - tsiviler ציוויילער
A civilian - a tsiviler אַ ציוויילער
Population - bafelkerung באַפעלקערונג
Socialism - satsyalizm סאָציאַליזם
Communism - komunizm קאָמוניזם
Racism - rasism ראַסיסם

Although he was the brutal dictator of the republic, in private he was a nice person.
khotsh er iz geven der brutal diktator fun der republik, in privat er iz geven a fayn mentsh.
כאָטש ער איז געווען דער ברוטאַל דיקטאַטאָר פון דער רעפּובליק, אין פּריוואַט ער
איז געווען אַ פֿײַנע מענטש.

In some countries torture and execution are common forms of legitimate punishment.
in etlekhe lender, paynikung aun ekzekutzia zenen a prost forem fun lajitamatzie shtrof.
אין עטלעכע לענדער, פּײַניקונג און עקזעקוציע זענען אַ פּראָסט פאָרעם פון
לאַדזשיטאַמאַציע שטראָף.

This is a violation of human rights and international law.
dos iz a khilel fun mentshnrekht aun internatsyonale gezets.
דאָס איז אַ חילול פון מענטשנרעכט און אינטערנאַציאָנאַלע געזעץ.

Communism and socialism were popular in the 19th century.
komunizm aun sotsyalizm zenen geven populer inem 19tn yorhundert.
קאָמוניזם און סאָציאַליזם זענען געווען פּאָפּולער אינעם 19טן יאָרהונדערט.

We support democracy and are against fascism and racism.
mir shtitsn demokrasi aun zenen kegn fashizam aun reysizam.
מיר שטיצן דעמאָקראַסי און זענען קעגן פאַשיזאַם און רייסיזאַם.

196

President - prezident פּרעזידענט

Presidential - presidentyal פּרעסידעננטיאַל

Vice president - vitse prezident וויצע פּרעזידענט

Defense minister - farteydikung minister פֿאַרטיידיקונג מיניסטער.

Interior minister - inern minister אינערן מיניסטער

Exterior minister - exteryor minister עקסטעריאָר מיניסטער

Prime minister - fremyer minister פּרעמיער מיניסטער

Democracy - demokratye דעמאָקראַטיע

Movement - bavegung באַוועגונג

Politician - falitiker פּאליטיקער

Politics - politik פּאָליטיק

To vote - tsu veilen צו וויילען

Independence - zelbstshtendikeyt זעלבסטשטענדיקייט

Party - fartey פּארטיי

Veto - Veto וועטאָ

Biased – pniusydik פּניותדיק

Resolution - hakhlote החלטה

Statement - derklerung דערקלערונג

They want to appoint him as defense minister.
zey viln im nominirn als farteydikung minister.
זיי ווילן אים נאָמינירן אלס פֿאַרטיידיקונג מיניסטער.

I want to see the presidential convoy.
ikh vil zen di prezadentshal kanvoy.
איך וויל זען די פּרעזאַדענטס קאַנוווי.

In some countries other than the United States, they have a prime minister, interior minister, and exterior minister.
in etlekhe lender aoyser di fareynigte shtatn habn zey a fremyer minister, inern minister aun exteryor minister.
אין עטלעכע לענדער אויסער די פאראייניגטע שטאַטן האבן זיי א פּרעמיער מיניסטער, אינערן מיניסטער און עקסטעריאָר מיניסטער.

I want to meet the president and the vice president.
ikh vil trefn dem frezident aun dem vitse frezident.
איך וויל טרעפֿן דעם פּרעזידענט און דעם וויצע פּרעזידענט.

The resolution is biased.
di hakhlote iz beyast.
די החלטה איז פּניותדיק

United Nations - fareynikte felker פֿאַרייניקטע פעלקער
United States - fareynigte shtatn פאראייניגטע שטאטן
European Union - eyrafeisher iunyan אייראפעישער יוניאַן
Military coup - militer ku מיליטער קו
Treason – far'rat פאררראט
Fascism - fashizm פאשיזם
Resistance - kegnshtel קעגנשטעל
Members - mitglider מיטגלידער
To capture - tsu khapn צו כאַפן
Rebels - rebeln רעבעלן
Condemnation - mshft משפט

All the members of the resistance were accused of treason and had to ask for political asylum.

di ale khbri m fu n de r vidershtan d zeyne n bashuldik t gevar n i n farrat, au n hab n gemuzt betn, falitish n asil.

די אלע חברים פו ן דער ווידערשטאנד זיינען באשולדיקט געוואָרן אין פאררראט, און האבן געמוזט בעטן, פאליטישן אסיל.

This was an official condemnation.

dos iz geven an afitsyele farmishpet

דאס איז געוווען אן אפיציעלע פארמשפט.

The United Nations is located in New York.

di fareynigte felker gefint zikh in niu yark.

די פאראייניגטע פעלקער געפינט זיך אין ניו יארק.

I am a United States citizen and a resident of the European Union.

ikh bin an amerikaner birger aun a toyshev fun di eyrafeishe iunyan.

איך בין אַן אמעריקאַנער בירגער און אַ תושב פון די אייראפעישע יוניאַן.

The international peace treaty needs to include both sides.

der internatsyanaler shlum afmakh darf areynnemen beyde zeytn.

דער אינטערנאציאנאלער שלום אפמאך דארף אריינגעמען ביידע זייטן.

According to the government, the rebels carried out an illegal military coup.

loyt der regirung, habn di rebeln durkhgefirt an aumlegale militerishe ku.

לויט דער רעגירונג, האבן די רעבעלן דורכגעפירט אן אומלעגאלע מיליטערישע קו.

MILITARY - MILITER מיליטער

Army - armey אַרמיי
War - mlkhmh מלחמה
Navy - navi נאַווי
Soldier - zelner זעלנער
A force - a kraft א קראַפט
Ground forces - erd forses ערד פאַרסעס
Base - baze באַזע
Headquarter - hoyptkvartir הויפטקווארטיר
Intelligence - inteligents אינטעליגענס
Ranks - reyen רייען
Sergeant - Sergent סערגעאַנט
Lieutenant - lutenant לוטענאַנט
The general - der general דע ר גענעראל
Commander - kamandir קאמאנדיר
Colonel - kalanel קאלאנעל
Chief of Staff - tshif fun shtab טשיף פון שטאב

I want to enlist in the military.
ikh vil zikh eynshreybn in militer.
איך וויל זיך איינשרייבן אין מיליטער.

This base is designated for military aircraft only.
di baze iz betzeichent bloyz far militerish luftshif
די באַזע איז באַצייכנט בלויז פאַר מיליטעריש לופטשיף

That is the headquarters of the enemy.
dos iz der hoyptkvartir fun di faynt.
דאָס איז דער הויפטקווארטיר פון די פײַנט.

The chief of staff was the target of a failed assassination attempt.
de r hoyft-shtab, iz geven der tsil, fun a durkhgefalener mard-pruve
דע הויפט־שטאב, איז געווען דער ציל, פון א דורכגעפאלענער מאַרד־פרוו.

The sniper killed the highest-ranking lieutenant.
der sneyfer hat aumgebrengt dem hekhstn loytenant.
דער סנייפער האט אומגעברענגט דעם העכסטן לויטענאַנט.

Refugee - plitim פּליטים
Camp - lager לאַגער
Reserves - rezerv רעזערוו
Terrorism - terorizm טעראָריזם
Terrorist - terorist טעראָריסט
Insurgency - inserjans אינסערדזשאַנס
Border crossing - grenets ariber גרענעץ אַריבער

They need to enlist reserve forces for the war.
zey darfn tsu arayntsyen rezerv forses far di mlkhmh.
זיי דאַרפֿן אַרייַנציען רעזערוו פֿאָרסעס פֿאַר די מלחמה.

Welcome to the border crossing.
brukhim habaim tsu der grenets aribergang.
ברוכים הבאים צו דער גרענעץ אַריבערגאַנג.

Military intelligence relies on important sources of information.
militer seykhl ferlozt zich aoyf vikhtike informatsye kvaln.
מיליטעריש שׂכל פֿאַרלאָזט זיך אויף וויכטיקע אינפֿאָרמאַציע קוואלן.

The terrorist group claimed responsibility for the car-bomb attack at the refugee camp.
di terar grufe hat genumen farantvartlikhkeyt far di kar-bambe atake inem flitim lager.
די טעראַר גרופֿע האָט גענומען פֿאַראַנטוואָרטליקקייט פֿאַר די קאַר-באָמבע אטאַקע אינעם פּליטים לאַגער.

It is impossible to defeat terrorism because it's an ideology.
es iz aummeglekh tsu bazign tererizam vayl es iz an ideologye.
עס איז אוממעגלעך צו באַזיגן טעררעריזם ווייל עס איז אַן אידעאָלאָגיע.

This country has a powerful airforce.
das land hat a shtarke luftflot fors.
דאַס לאַנד האָט אַ שטאַרקע לופֿטפֿלאָט

200

A target - a tsil א ציל

To target - tsu tsiln צו צילן

Intense - intensive אינטענסיווע

To shoot - tsu shisn צו שיסן

Open fire - efenen feyer עפענען פייער

Fired - feyerd פייערד

Assassination - asasaneyshan אסאסאניישאן

Assassin - merder מערדער

Enemy - faynt פײַנט

Reconnaissance - rekonnaissanse רעקאָננאַיסאַנסע

To infiltrate - tsu infiltrirn צו אינפילטרירן

Invasion - invazye אינוואַזיע

There is an invasion of ground forces.

es iz a invazye fun erd forses.

.עס איז אַן אינוואַזיע פון ערד פאָרסעס

The soldier wanted to open fire and shoot at the enemy.

der saldat hat gevalt efen feyer aun shisn, aoyf di invadatsye-khukhus.

.דער סאלדאט האט געוואלט עפענען פייער און שיסן אויף די שונאים

The bomb attack was considered as an act of aggression and an act of war.

d i bambe-atake iz batrakht gevarn altz an anfalg aun a milkhama-akt.

די באמבע-אטאקע איז באטראכט געווארן אלץ אן אנפאלג און א מלחמה-אקט

The mortar attack and exchange of fire caused injuries and deaths on both sides.

di morter atake aun aoystoysh fun feyer habn faraurzakht vaundn aun toyte fun beyde zeytn.

די מאָרטער אטאקע און אויסטויש פון פייער האבן פאראורזאכט וואונדן און טויטע
.פון ביידע זייטן

Exchange of fire - aoystoysh fun feyer אויסטויש פון פייער
A cease fire - a feyer aoyfher א פייער אויפהער
To win - tsu gevinen צו געווינען
To surrender - tsu aroysgebn צו אַרויסגעבן
Victim - korbn קרבן
Injured - farvaundet פֿאַרוואונדעט
Deaths - toyte טויטע
Killed - derhrget דערהרגעט
To kill - tsu teytn צו טייטן
Prisoner of war - gefangene fun krig געפֿאַנגענע פון קריג
Missing in action - felndik in kamf פֿעלנדיק אין קאַמף
Act of war - akt fun mlkhmh אקט פון מלחמה
War crimes - mlkhmh kreymz מלחמה קריימז
Defense - farteydikung פֿאַרטיידיקונג
Attempt - pruvun פרווון
An attack - an atak אַן אַטאַק
To attack - tsu bafaln צו באַפֿאַלן

The ceasefire agreement included the release of prisoners of war.
der aoyfher afmakh hat areyngerekhnt di bafreytung fun krigs-
gefangene.
דער אויפהער אפמאך האט אריינגערעכנט די באפרייטונג פון קריגס-געפֿאַנגענע.

The army made a public statement to announce the withdrawal.
di armey hat gemakht a fublik steitment tsu meldn dem tsuriktsyen.
די ארמיי האט געמאכט א פובליק סטעיטמענט צו מעלדן דעם צוריקציען.

There was a huge explosion as a result of the terrorist attack.
es iz geven a rizik oifrays altz rezultat fun di terorist bafal.
עס איז געווען אַ ריזיק אויפרייס אלץ רעזולטאט פון די טעראָריסט באפֿאַלן.

The commander of the insurgency was accused of serious war crimes.
der kamandir fun di aoyfshtand iz bashuldigt gevarn in ernste mlkhmh
farbrekhns.
דער קאמאנדיר פון די אויפשטאנד איז באשולדיגט געוואָרן אין ערנסטע מלחמה פֿאַרברעכנס.

Several of the submarine sailors were missing in action.
etlekhe fun di submarin seylerz zenen felndik in kamf.
עטלעכע פון די סובמאַרין סיילערז זענען פעלנדיק אין קאַמף.

Conclusion

Hopefully, you have enjoyed this book and will use the knowledge you have learned in various situations in your everyday life. In contrast to other methods of learning foreign languages, the theory in this current usage is that ever-greater topics can be broached so that one's vocabulary can expand. This method relies on the discovery I made of the list of core words from each language. Once these are learned, your conversational learning skills will progress very quickly.

You are now ready to discuss sport and school and office-related topics and this will open up your world to a more satisfying extent. Humans are social creatures and language helps us interact. Indeed, at times, it can keep us alive, such as in war situations. You might find yourself in dangerous situations perhaps as a journalist, military personnel or civilian and you need to be armed with the appropriate vocabulary.

"This is a base for military aircraft only," you may have to tell some people who try to enter a field you are protecting, or know what you are being told when someone says to you, "Welcome to the border crossing." As a journalist on a foreign assignment, you may need to quickly understand what you are being told, such as "The sniper killed the highest-ranking lieutenant." If you are someone negotiating on behalf of the army, you may need to find another lieutenant very quickly. Lives, at times, literally depend on your level of understanding and comprehension.

This unique approach that I first discovered when using this method to learn on my own, will have helped you speak the Yiddish language much quicker than any other way.

Congratulations! Now You Are on Your Own!

If you merely absorb the required words in this book, you will then have acquired the basis to become conversational in Yiddish! After memorizing these words, this conversational foundational basis that you have just gained will trigger your ability to make improvements in conversational fluency at an amazing speed! However, in order to engage in quick and easy conversational communication, you need a special type of basics, and this book will provide you with just that.

Unlike the foreign language learning systems presently used in schools and universities, along with books and programs that are available on the market today, that focus on *everything* but being conversational, *this* method's sole focus is on becoming conversational in Yiddish as well as any other language. Once you have successfully mastered the required words in this book, there are two techniques that if combined with these essential words, can further enhance your skills and will result in you improving your proficiency tenfold. *However*, these two techniques will only succeed *if* you have completely and successfully absorbed these required words. *After* you establish the basis for fluent communications by memorizing these words, you can enhance your conversational abilities even more if you use the following two techniques.

The first step is to attend a Yiddish language class that will enable you to sharpen your grammar. You will gain additional vocabulary and learn past and present tenses, and if you apply these skills that you learn in the class, together with these words that you have previously memorized, you will be improving your conversational skills tenfold. You will notice that, conversationally, you will succeed at a much higher rate than any of your classmates.

Once you have established a basis of quick and easy conversation in Yiddish with those words that you just attained, every additional word or grammar rule you pick up from there on will be gravy. And these additional words or grammar rules can be combined with the these words, enriching your conversational abilities even more. Basically, after the research and studies I've conducted with my method over the years, I came to the conclusion that in order to become conversational, you first must learn the words and *then* learn the grammar.

The Yiddish language is compatible with the mirror translation technique. Likewise, with *this* language, you can use this mirror translation technique in order to become conversational, enabling you to communicate even more effortlessly. Mirror translation is the method of translating a phrase or sentence, word for word from English to Yiddish, by using these imperative words that you have acquired through this program (such as the sentences I used in this book). Latin languages, Middle Eastern languages, and Slavic languages, along with a few others, are also compatible with the mirror translation technique. Though you won't be speaking perfectly proper and precise Yiddish, you will still be fully understood and, conversation-wise, be able to get by just fine.

NOTE FROM THE AUTHOR

Thank you for your interest in my work. I encourage you to share your overall experience of this book by posting a review. Your review can make a difference! Please feel free to describe how you benefited from my method or provide creative feedback on how I can improve this program. I am constantly seeking ways to enhance the quality of this product, based on personal testimonials and suggestions from individuals like you. In order to post a review, please check with the retailer of this book.

Thanks and best of luck,

Yatir Nitzany

Made in the USA
Middletown, DE
09 September 2024

60611555R00115